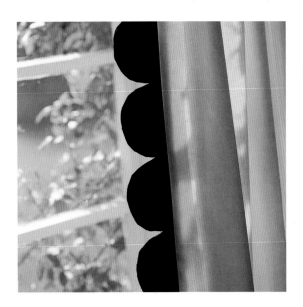

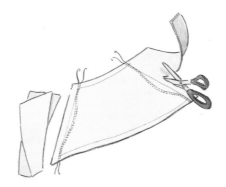

the home furnishing workbook

Katrin Cargill

photography by James Merrell

RYLAND
PETERS
& SMALL

LONDON NEW YORK

First published in the United States
in 1999, this edition published in 2006
by Ryland Peters & Small
519 Broadway, 5th Floor
New York, NY 10012
10 9 8 7 6 5 4 3 2 1
Text © Katrin Cargill 1996, 1998, 1999, and 2006.
Design and photographs © Ryland Peters & Small
1996, 1998, 1999, and 2006.

Printed in China

ISBN-10: 1 84597 122 1
ISBN-13: 978 1 84597 122 9

Catalog-in-Publication Data is available from the
Library of Congress on request.

Senior designers Paul Tilby and Larraine Shamwana
Designers Sally Powell and Ingunn Jensen
Senior editors Annabel Morgan and Sian Parkhouse
Editors Maddalena Bastianelli, Toria Leitch, and
Sophie Pearse
Design assistants Luis Peral-Aranda and Mark Latter
Production Manager Patricia Harrington

Illustrators Michael Hill, Jacqueline Pestell,
and Lizzie Sanders

The material contained in this book was originally
published in four different titles: *Lampshades* and
Pillows (both published in 1996) and *Simple Beds*
and *Simple Curtains* (both published in 1998).

contents

Luckily, the recent trend toward less cluttered, busy interiors means we no longer need to spend a fortune buying yards of fabric to festoon our homes. Nowadays, clean lines, appealing textures, and strong colors make a much more sophisticated statement than acres of stiff brocade, rows of flouncy frills, or overelaborate trimmings. Grandeur and formality have made way for a new, inviting mood of simplicity and freshness.

However, if this new look of understated elegance is to be effective, it does demand a certain amount of attention to detail, quality, and finish. You may need less fabric to make these new home furnishings, but because the items are more simple and unadorned, the fabric should be the very best you can afford, in exactly the right color and texture for your room. And just a few finishing touches—the special trimming on a lampshade, perhaps, or velvet piping on a pillow—will turn a humble homemade item into a piece of furnishing haute couture.

Another important factor is choosing exactly the right curtain, bedspread, lampshade, or pillow for your room. Try to be sensitive to the dimensions and proportions of your home. In a tiny space, allow understated but elegant drapes or a luxurious bedspread to be the single central focus. In a larger room, you can afford to add a few more elements—combine a couple of plump, inviting pillows with well-chosen lampshades and a pair of softly gathered curtains to enliven your interior.

In this book, I have put together a collection of varied ideas to inspire you to create elegant and stylish rooms. There are hundreds of imaginative suggestions for you to make at home, whatever your level of skill, and 32 fully illustrated projects that clearly explain how to achieve entirely professional results. These projects can easily be adapted to suit your own color scheme or scaled up or down to suit the proportions of your home.

The key message in all the projects and ideas is to keep them simple and pay attention to detail and quality—it is far better to make a plain pillow in a wonderfully luxurious fabric than to complicate it by adding overambitious trimmings or an excess of details. By the same token, the effect on a room of a pair of unlined curtains in a heavy, good-quality fabric, hung from a sturdy wooden or metal pole, is far superior to heavily lined and interlined drapes with ornate valances and swags and tails, which will only catch the dust and dirt and are horribly difficult to clean.

Happy sewing and decorating!
Katrin Cargill

bed linen

pillows and sheets

A bedroom is a place for sleep, but it is also a room where you can be a little self–indulgent with your forms of decoration. Don't just stick to the usual plain bed dressings, but instead use checks or stripes to add a simple yet eye–catching area of interest. If this seems too adventurous, introduce more subtle decorative touches, such as an embroidered or contrasting border running around the edges of sheets, or ties and buttoning on pillows.

far left *The simple geometric designs of the decorative stitching on these pillowcases perfectly complements the colors and shapes of the patchwork bedspread.*
center *Delicate white thread embroidery enlivens the edges of a crisp cotton sheet and matching pillowcase.*
left *The regimented stripes and precisely squared ends of this plump bolster are the perfect match for the bedspread beneath, giving the bed an air of tailored elegance.*
below left *Using ties as a fastening is a simple solution to closing covers and cases as well as an attractive decorative addition. Either make them in a contrasting fabric or use the same material for a more subtle form of embellishment.*
below right *Checks and stripes in combination are unified by the use of a blue and white color scheme throughout.*

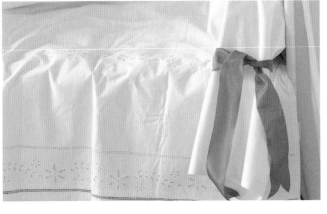

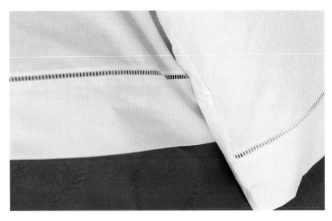

top left *An impromptu bolster case is constructed from a piece of white cotton loosely tied with a peach satin ribbon.*
top right *A dainty drawn threadwork border embellishes these matching pillowcases. The crisp cool cotton of the bed linen is teamed with a vivid red bedspread for a cozy countrified effect.*
above left *A hot pink flanged border adds a bold and colorful note to an otherwise plain pair of white pillowcases.*
above right *Quilted fabric with an unusual textural quality adds interest to a pillow and creates a cozy comfortable feel.*
far left *Linen pillowcases and sheets are the ultimate luxury. This linen pillowcase is held closed by floppy linen bows; a soft, informal look perfect for a bedroom.*
left *Lacy delicate cutwork on starched white cotton is a bed linen lassic. Here, a pretty daisy pattern adorns the border of a large square pillowcase.*

piqué pillows with bows

These invitingly plump brown gingham pillowcases are extremely easy to make, especially if you use extra-wide sheeting fabric, as you will need only a single piece of fabric that is twice the width of the pillow. The piqué panels, held in place with matching gingham bows, lend the pillowcases a demure air of modesty and old-fashioned charm.

materials & equipment

cotton gingham fabric
cotton piqué fabric

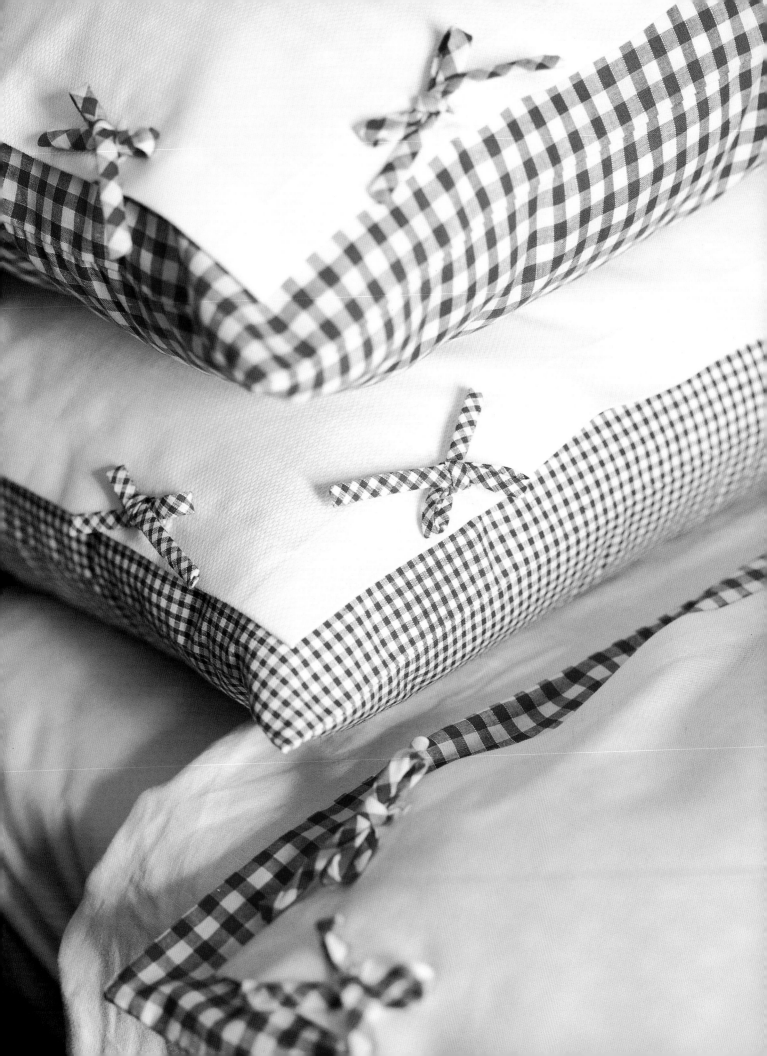

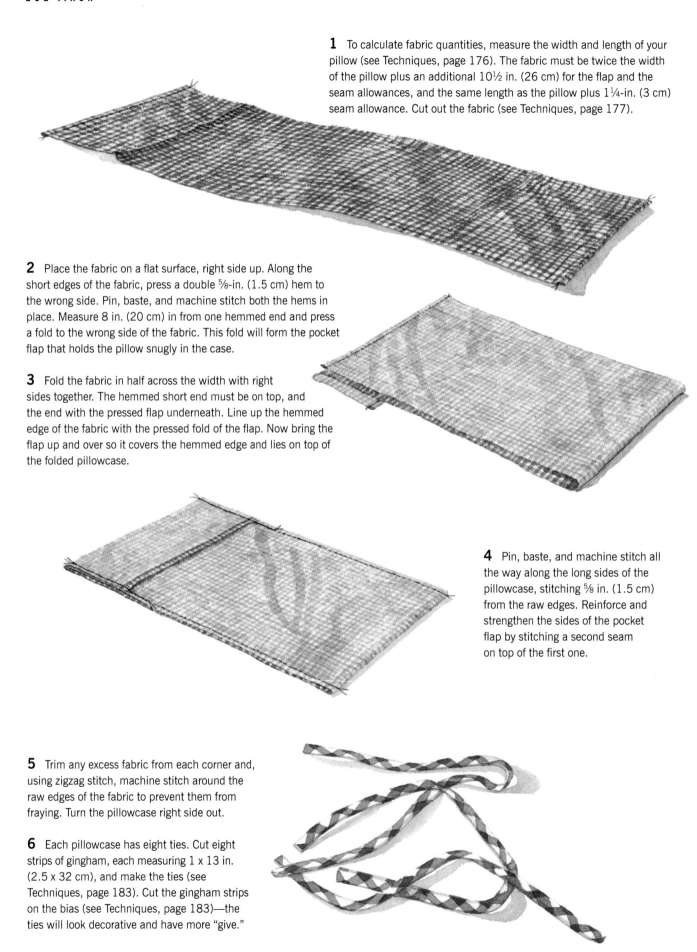

1 To calculate fabric quantities, measure the width and length of your pillow (see Techniques, page 176). The fabric must be twice the width of the pillow plus an additional 10½ in. (26 cm) for the flap and the seam allowances, and the same length as the pillow plus 1¼-in. (3 cm) seam allowance. Cut out the fabric (see Techniques, page 177).

2 Place the fabric on a flat surface, right side up. Along the short edges of the fabric, press a double ⅝-in. (1.5 cm) hem to the wrong side. Pin, baste, and machine stitch both the hems in place. Measure 8 in. (20 cm) in from one hemmed end and press a fold to the wrong side of the fabric. This fold will form the pocket flap that holds the pillow snugly in the case.

3 Fold the fabric in half across the width with right sides together. The hemmed short end must be on top, and the end with the pressed flap underneath. Line up the hemmed edge of the fabric with the pressed fold of the flap. Now bring the flap up and over so it covers the hemmed edge and lies on top of the folded pillowcase.

4 Pin, baste, and machine stitch all the way along the long sides of the pillowcase, stitching ⅝ in. (1.5 cm) from the raw edges. Reinforce and strengthen the sides of the pocket flap by stitching a second seam on top of the first one.

5 Trim any excess fabric from each corner and, using zigzag stitch, machine stitch around the raw edges of the fabric to prevent them from fraying. Turn the pillowcase right side out.

6 Each pillowcase has eight ties. Cut eight strips of gingham, each measuring 1 x 13 in. (2.5 x 32 cm), and make the ties (see Techniques, page 183). Cut the gingham strips on the bias (see Techniques, page 183)—the ties will look decorative and have more "give."

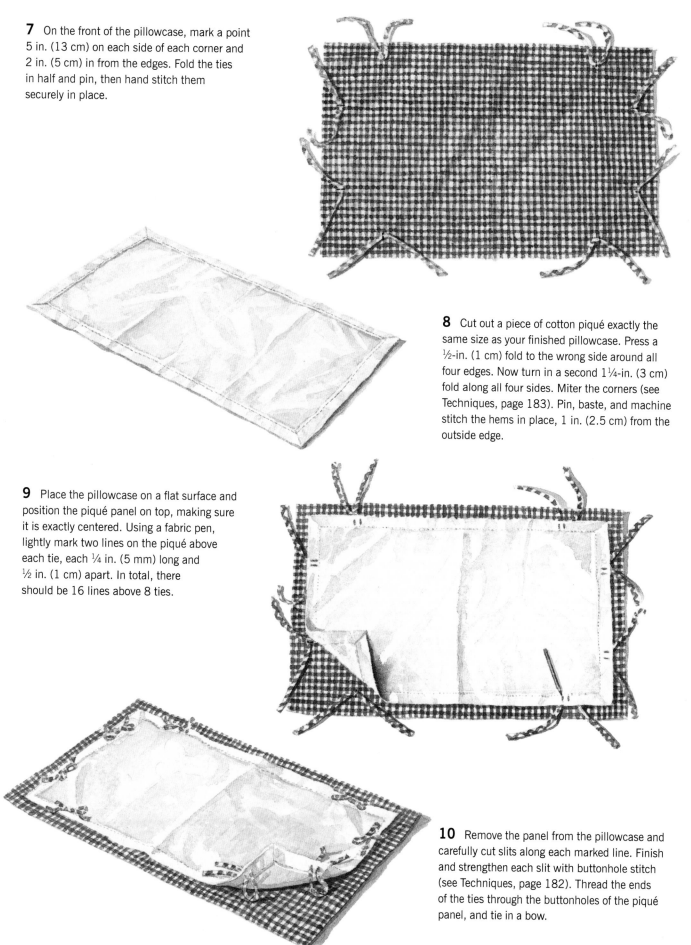

7 On the front of the pillowcase, mark a point 5 in. (13 cm) on each side of each corner and 2 in. (5 cm) in from the edges. Fold the ties in half and pin, then hand stitch them securely in place.

8 Cut out a piece of cotton piqué exactly the same size as your finished pillowcase. Press a ½-in. (1 cm) fold to the wrong side around all four edges. Now turn in a second 1¼-in. (3 cm) fold along all four sides. Miter the corners (see Techniques, page 183). Pin, baste, and machine stitch the hems in place, 1 in. (2.5 cm) from the outside edge.

9 Place the pillowcase on a flat surface and position the piqué panel on top, making sure it is exactly centered. Using a fabric pen, lightly mark two lines on the piqué above each tie, each ¼ in. (5 mm) long and ½ in. (1 cm) apart. In total, there should be 16 lines above 8 ties.

10 Remove the panel from the pillowcase and carefully cut slits along each marked line. Finish and strengthen each slit with buttonhole stitch (see Techniques, page 182). Thread the ends of the ties through the buttonholes of the piqué panel, and tie in a bow.

red-trimmed linen

Cool linen sheets and pillowcases are irresistibly inviting after a long day. Here, square pillows have been encased in linen pillowcases trimmed with boldly colored faggoting for a cozy, country effect. Teamed with a matching sheet and a simple gingham bedspread, they bring a charming air of simplicity to a bedroom.

materials & equipment

white cotton or linen fabric

¾-in. (2 cm) wide trim

1 The back panel is made from two pieces of fabric. Measure the pillow and add 8 in. (20 cm) to the width and the length. Add a further 5 in. (12 cm) to the width. Divide this measurement by two to calculate the size of each piece.

2 Cut out the back panels. Press a ½-in. (1 cm) single hem along one long side of each panel. Pin, baste, and machine stitch in place. Place the panels on a flat surface, right sides together and hemmed edges aligned. Seam the hemmed sides, 2 in. (5 cm) in from the hemmed edge. Leave a 16-in. (40 cm) opening in the center of the seam. Open out and press the seam.

3 For the central panel, cut out a square of fabric the same size as the pillow plus a ½-in. (1 cm) seam allowance all around. Press a ½-in. (1 cm) hem around all four edges.

4 Cut out four strips of trim, each one ¾ in. (2 cm) longer than the sides of the central panel minus the seam allowance.

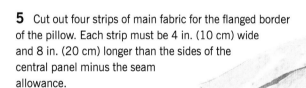

5 Cut out four strips of main fabric for the flanged border of the pillow. Each strip must be 4 in. (10 cm) wide and 8 in. (20 cm) longer than the sides of the central panel minus the seam allowance.

6 Place two border strips right sides together. Pin and baste the strips together at a 45° angle from the top corner. Check that the angle of the seam is correct; then machine stitch, stopping ⅝ in. (1.5 cm) from the bottom of the strip. Attach the other strips in the same way until the border is complete. Press open the seams, then press a ⅝-in. (1.5 cm) hem to the wrong side all around the inside of the border.

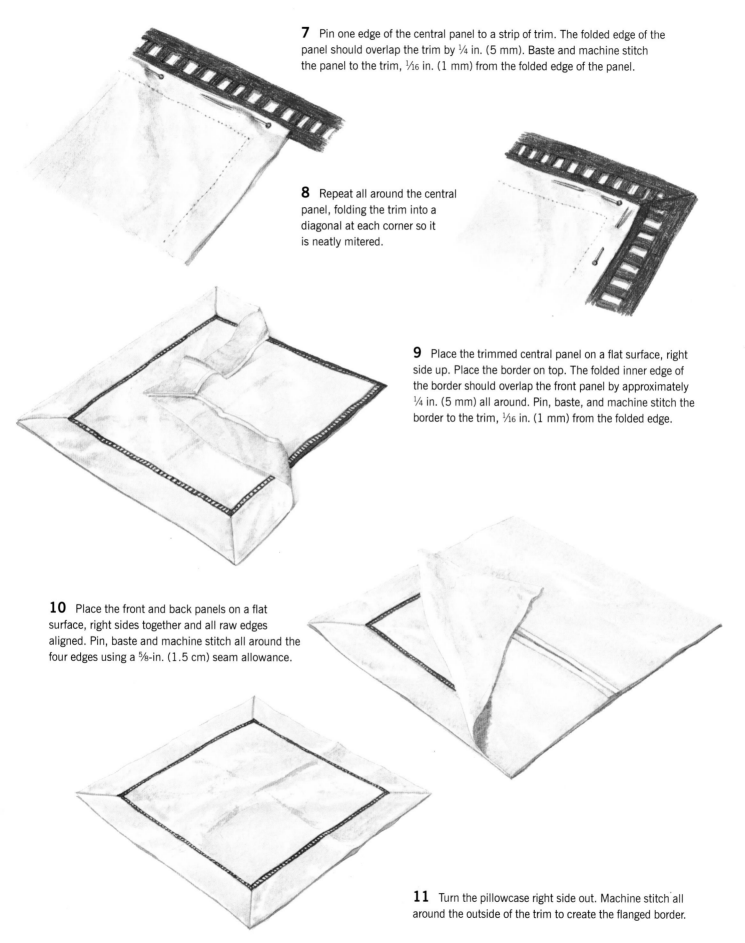

7 Pin one edge of the central panel to a strip of trim. The folded edge of the panel should overlap the trim by ¼ in. (5 mm). Baste and machine stitch the panel to the trim, ¹⁄₁₆ in. (1 mm) from the folded edge of the panel.

8 Repeat all around the central panel, folding the trim into a diagonal at each corner so it is neatly mitered.

9 Place the trimmed central panel on a flat surface, right side up. Place the border on top. The folded inner edge of the border should overlap the front panel by approximately ¼ in. (5 mm) all around. Pin, baste, and machine stitch the border to the trim, ¹⁄₁₆ in. (1 mm) from the folded edge.

10 Place the front and back panels on a flat surface, right sides together and all raw edges aligned. Pin, baste and machine stitch all around the four edges using a ⅝-in. (1.5 cm) seam allowance.

11 Turn the pillowcase right side out. Machine stitch all around the outside of the trim to create the flanged border.

bedspreads

Bedspreads have a dual function—to provide warmth and decoration. Whether your preference is for dainty florals or bold tailored stripes, your bedspread must be both attractive and inviting, and its fabric and design should suggest comfort and a hint of luxury.

bottom left *A floral cotton sheet with a ruffled border makes a pretty summer bedspread.*
bottom right *A bold black and ecru checked eiderdown creates a cozy yet entirely contemporary effect.*

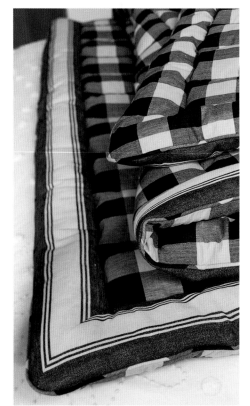

above far left *Graphic stripes and unusual surface texturing enhance a simple sleigh bed.*
above center left *A complementary colored checked border and a matching appliquéd crown motif give an old wool blanket a new lease on life.*
above center right *Crocheted cotton bedspreads are available in a wide range of patterns and colors. This is a fine example of intricate white-on-white crochet work, topped with a cotton bolster.*
above far right *A plump feather eiderdown covered in a cheerful check makes a snug and warm winter bedspread. The channel quilting holds the filling in place and prevents any lumping.*

above left *Quilted blue and white checks are smartly teamed with toning ticking.*

above center *A crisp white cotton bedspread made from Marseilles cloth. Jacquard would create a similar effect.*

above right *A faded country quilt to snuggle up beneath.*

left *A wool blanket embellished with decorative embroidery and a loopy trim.*

right *An antique floral eiderdown with an enticing air of cosiness and comfort.*

bottom left *Delicate lace work has an air of distinction.*

above right *This colorful bedspread is cleverly constructed from remnants of antique ticking.*

appliquéd quilted bedspread

This stylish double bedspread is made from matelasse, a thick double cloth with a quilted effect. A crisp blue-striped ribbon has been appliquéd to the bedspread in a bold and geometric pattern of squares. It is essential that the bedspread itself is an exact square, so no unevenly sized squares or crooked lines can mar its perfection.

materials & equipment

85 x 85 in. (220 x 220 cm) matelasse fabric

28½ yd. (27 m) striped ribbon

1 Cut out the fabric and join widths if necessary, using a flat fell seam (see Techniques, page 183). Make sure you have a full-width panel set in the center of the bedspread with equal part-widths on each side.

2 Cut the blue-striped ribbon into 12 equal lengths of exactly 85 in. (220 cm) each.

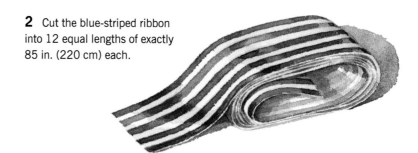

3 Lay the bedspread on a flat surface, right side up. Mark a line running the whole length of the bedspread, 17 in. (44 cm) from the left-hand side of the fabric.

4 Mark three more vertical lines across the fabric at 17-in. (44 cm) intervals. The last line should be 17 in. (44 cm) from the right-hand side of the bedspread.

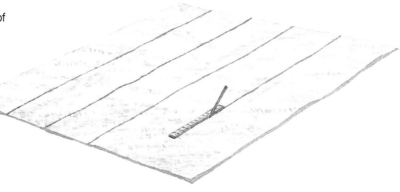

5 Still working on the right side of the bedspread, mark a horizontal line 17 in. (44 cm) down from the top edge of the bedspread. Mark another three lines at 17-in. (44 cm) intervals down the bedspread. Use a drawing square to check that the horizontal lines are at an exact 90˚ angle to the vertical stripes.

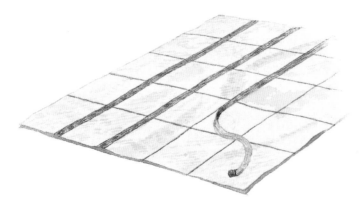

6 Take the first length of ribbon and place it on top of the bedspread, the left-hand edge of the ribbon aligned with the first vertical line running down the bedspread. Pin and baste in place down the length of the bedspread. Repeat across the bedspread until there are 4 lengths of ribbon basted vertically in place.

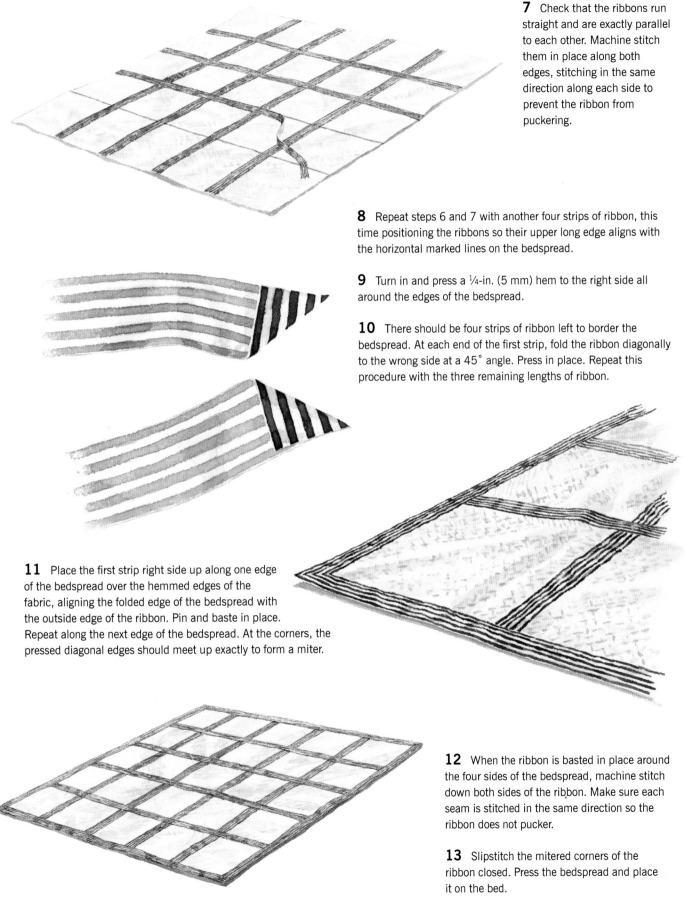

7 Check that the ribbons run straight and are exactly parallel to each other. Machine stitch them in place along both edges, stitching in the same direction along each side to prevent the ribbon from puckering.

8 Repeat steps 6 and 7 with another four strips of ribbon, this time positioning the ribbons so their upper long edge aligns with the horizontal marked lines on the bedspread.

9 Turn in and press a ¼-in. (5 mm) hem to the right side all around the edges of the bedspread.

10 There should be four strips of ribbon left to border the bedspread. At each end of the first strip, fold the ribbon diagonally to the wrong side at a 45˚ angle. Press in place. Repeat this procedure with the three remaining lengths of ribbon.

11 Place the first strip right side up along one edge of the bedspread over the hemmed edges of the fabric, aligning the folded edge of the bedspread with the outside edge of the ribbon. Pin and baste in place. Repeat along the next edge of the bedspread. At the corners, the pressed diagonal edges should meet up exactly to form a miter.

12 When the ribbon is basted in place around the four sides of the bedspread, machine stitch down both sides of the ribbon. Make sure each seam is stitched in the same direction so the ribbon does not pucker.

13 Slipstitch the mitered corners of the ribbon closed. Press the bedspread and place it on the bed.

feather-stitched patchwork quilt

This cozy patchwork quilt, made from scraps and remnants of antique blue and white printed cotton, is not handstitched in the traditional way. Instead, the quilt is machine sewn to save time and effort. Feather stitching in a complementary color meanders over and around the seams, providing a decorative finishing touch.

materials & equipment

a wide variety of scraps and remnants of fabric for the patchwork batting

backing fabric for the quilt

embroidery needle

embroidery thread

1 Measure your bed (see Techniques, page 176) to calculate how much fabric you will need. The backing fabric and the finished piece of patchwork must be the size of the finished quilt plus ¾ in. (2 cm) added all around. The batting must also be the size of the finished quilt but without seam allowances.

2 Each patchwork square is 4 x 4 in. (10 x 10 cm) plus an additional ½-in. (1 cm) seam allowance. To work out how many squares you will need for the quilt, divide the width and the length of the finished quilt by 4 (or 10 if you are using cms). To calculate how many squares you will need in total, multiply the number of squares that will run across the quilt by the number that will run down the quilt.

3 Make a square cardboard template measuring 4½ x 4½ in. (11 x 11 cm).

4 Amass your scraps and remnants of fabric. Place the template on the wrong side of a scrap. Mark around it, then remove it. Cut out the square. Position your template carefully to get as many squares as possible from each piece of material.

5 When you have cut out the requisite number of squares, place two squares right sides together. Pin, baste, and machine stitch down one side, using a ¼-in. (5 mm) seam allowance. Press the seam flat. Add another square to one of the attached squares. Continue until you have a strip of squares the same width as your bedspread.

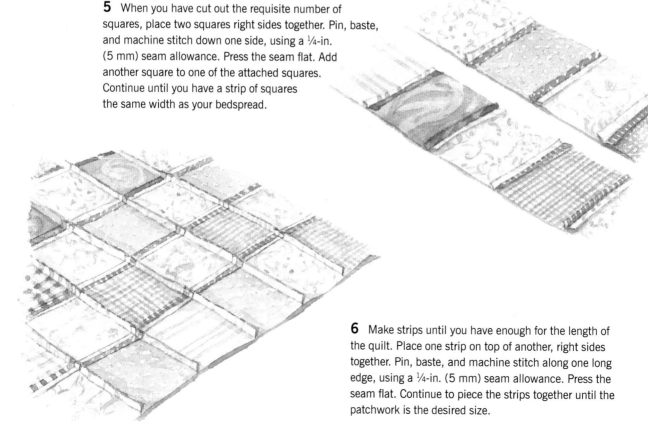

6 Make strips until you have enough for the length of the quilt. Place one strip on top of another, right sides together. Pin, baste, and machine stitch along one long edge, using a ¼-in. (5 mm) seam allowance. Press the seam flat. Continue to piece the strips together until the patchwork is the desired size.

7 Lay the finished piece of patchwork on a flat surface, right side down. Place the batting on top, aligning all raw edges. Pin, baste, and machine stitch around the sides of the batting, using a ½-in. (1 cm) seam allowance. Run a line of stitching down and across some of the seams of the patchwork to hold the batting in place.

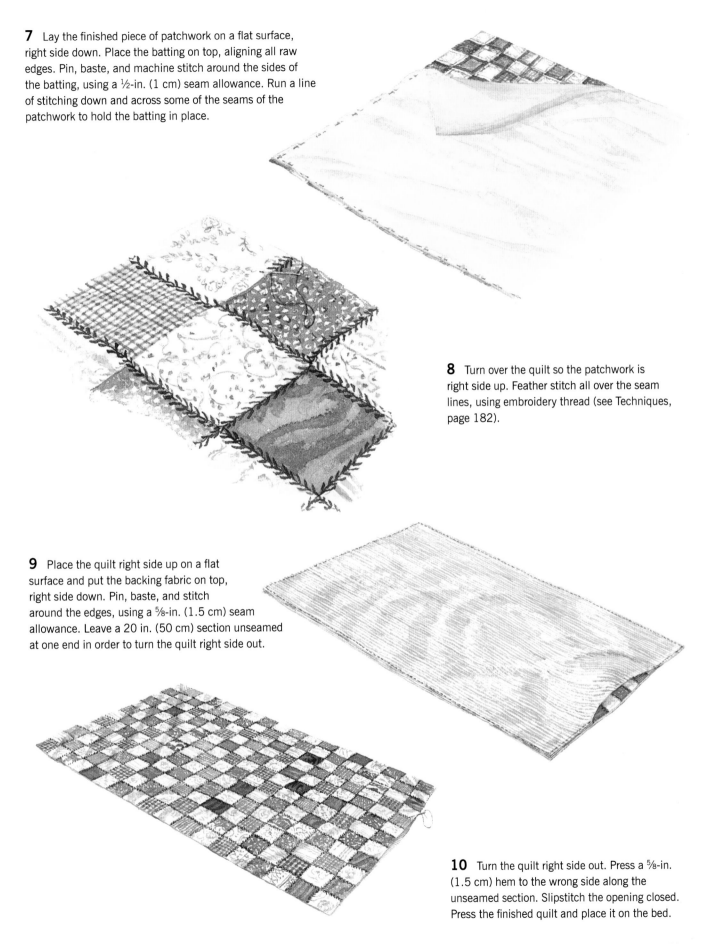

8 Turn over the quilt so the patchwork is right side up. Feather stitch all over the seam lines, using embroidery thread (see Techniques, page 182).

9 Place the quilt right side up on a flat surface and put the backing fabric on top, right side down. Pin, baste, and stitch around the edges, using a ⅝-in. (1.5 cm) seam allowance. Leave a 20 in. (50 cm) section unseamed at one end in order to turn the quilt right side out.

10 Turn the quilt right side out. Press a ⅝-in. (1.5 cm) hem to the wrong side along the unseamed section. Slipstitch the opening closed. Press the finished quilt and place it on the bed.

dust ruffles

Dust ruffles serve a practical purpose, concealing unattractive bed bases, stumpy bed legs, and underbed storage areas. Overelaborate specimens made in flouncy, fussy designs have earned dust ruffles a bad reputation. However, it is undeserved, for a tailored example with inverted pleats can be extremely elegant, while a delicate lace–trimmed one made from antique cotton sheets will add distinction to any bedroom.

left and far left *Fine organza with a deep double hem billows out beneath a simple wooden–framed bed. Despite its fragile, flimsy appearance, organza is extremely strong, making it a luxurious yet practical choice for soft furnishings.*
below *In a guest bedroom, a blue and white theme boldly combines checks, stripes, and flowers, and demonstrates how different patterns can be harmoniously linked by color alone. This stylish effect has been achieved on a tight budget—the dust ruffles are fashioned from humble dish towels.*
opposite above right and below right *A colorful red and white checked cotton is sewn into precise box pleats in this cheerful dust ruffle, which makes the bed the focal point in this small bedroom.*
opposite above left *A simple yet sophisticated linen dust ruffle with an inverted pleat at the corners adds a unfussy note of comfort to a cool contemporary interior.*

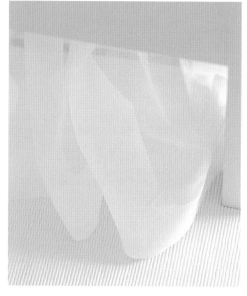

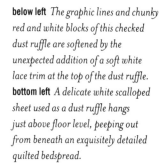

below left *The graphic lines and chunky red and white blocks of this checked dust ruffle are softened by the unexpected addition of a soft white lace trim at the top of the dust ruffle.*
bottom left *A delicate white scalloped sheet used as a dust ruffle hangs just above floor level, peeping out from beneath an exquisitely detailed quilted bedspread.*

tailored pictorial print

Toile de Jouy, a cotton fabric printed with idyllic pastoral scenes in muted tones, is ideally suited to a relaxed and soothing bedroom environment. If it is made into frilly bed dressings, the effect can be a little too "cute." However, *toile de Jouy* is ideally suited to the simple uncluttered lines of this chic, precisely pleated dust ruffle.

materials & equipment

toile de Jouy *fabric*

lining fabric

cording

bias binding (the same color as the piping cord)

1 To calculate fabric quantities, measure the bed (see Techniques, page 176). The skirt is made from five pieces of fabric. Cut two side panels, the length of the bed plus 6 in. (15 cm) and an end panel, equal to the width of the bed plus 12 in. (30 cm). Add ⅝-in. (1.5 cm) seam allowance to the length. Cut two pieces of fabric for the pleats, each 12 in. (30 cm) long and the height of the side and end panels.

2 The central panel of the dust ruffle, which is concealed by the mattress, is made of lining fabric bordered with *toile de Jouy*. For the lining panel, deduct 12 in. (30 cm) from the length and width of the bed base. Cut out the lining to these measurements, joining widths if necessary (see Techniques, page 177).

3 To border the lining panel, cut four strips of toile, two 7-in. (18 cm) wide and the same length as the bed base plus 2 in. (5 cm) and two 7-in. (18 cm) wide and equal to the width of the bed base plus 2 in. (5 cm).

4 Place a long and a short border strip right sides together, all raw edges aligned. Pin and baste the strips together at a 45° angle running diagonally down from the top corner. Check that the angle of the seam is correct, then machine stitch. Stop stitching ⅝ in. (1.5 cm) from the bottom edge of the strip. Attach the other strips in the same way until the border is complete. Press the seams open then press a ⅝-in. (1.5 cm) fold to the wrong side all around the inside edge of the border.

5 Place the central lining panel right side up on a flat surface and lay the border over it, also right side up, making sure the edges overlap evenly all around. Pin, baste, and machine stitch the border to the central panel. At the top (head) end of the border, press a double ¼-in. (5 mm) hem.

6 Take the three pieces of fabric for the skirt and the two narrower pieces of fabric for the inverted pleats. With right sides together, join one side of each corner pleat to a side panel, then the other side of the corner pleat to an end panel. Pin, baste, and machine stitch in place.

7 Make a strip of bias binding equal in length to the bottom edge of the joined skirt (see Techniques, page 183). Press a ¼-in. (5 mm) fold to the wrong side along both long edges, then press the strips in half so the folded edges meet.

8 Insert the bottom raw edge of the skirt into the folded bias binding. Pin, baste, and machine stitch the binding in place along both sides of the bottom edge of the skirt, close to the folded edge of the binding.

9 Mark a line 5½ in. (14 cm) to each side of the pleat panels. Fold the end and side panels along these lines so they meet over the pleat sections. Pin, then baste the pleats in place.

10 Make a length of cording equal to the top edge of the skirt.

11 Place the central panel on a flat surface and pin the cording around the sides and unhemmed end of the central panel, aligning all raw edges.

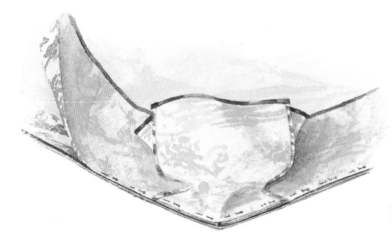

12 Place the skirt on the central panel, right side down, all raw edges aligned and the pleats positioned exactly at the corners of the main panel. The piping should be sandwiched between the two. Pin, baste, and machine stitch a seam ⅝-in. (1.5 cm) from the raw edges, making sure the piping cord is on the inside of the stitching.

13 Press the finished dust ruffle and place it on the bed base.

appliquéd zigzags

This bold dust ruffle strikes a note of warmth and vitality. The hot pink color and solid shapes of the skirt are a perfect foil for the graceful fluid outline of an antique brass bedstead. A down-home check fabric, which harmonizes perfectly with the pink of the skirt, has been used for the duvet and cut into squares that are applied to the skirt on point to make diamonds.

materials & equipment

plain cotton fabric

checked cotton or gingham

lining fabric

1 To calculate fabric quantities, measure the bed (see Techniques, page 176). The skirt of the dust ruffle is made from three pieces of fabric. Cut two side panels the length of the sides of the bed, and one end panel the width of the end of the bed. Add a ⅝-in. (1.5 cm) seam allowance to the depth of the skirt.

2 The central panel of the dust ruffle, which is concealed by the mattress, is made of lining fabric bordered with main fabric. For the lining panel, deduct 12 in. (30 cm) from the length and width of the bed base. Cut out the lining fabric to these measurements. Join widths if necessary (see Techniques, page 177).

3 To border the central lining panel, cut four strips of main fabric, two of them 7 in. (18 cm) wide and the same length as the sides of the bed base plus 2 in. (5 cm), and the other two 7 in. (18 cm) wide and the same width as the ends of the bed base plus 2 in. (5 cm).

4 Place a long and a short strip right sides together. Pin and baste the strips together at a 45° angle from the top corner. Check that the angle is correct, then machine stitch, stopping ⅝ in. (1.5 cm) from the bottom of the strip. Attach the other strips until the border is complete. Press open the seams, then press a ⅝-in. (1.5 cm) fold to the wrong side all around the inside edge of the border.

5 Place the lining panel right side up with the border on top, right side up. Make sure the edges overlap evenly all around. Pin, baste, and machine stitch the two together. At the top (head) end, press a double ¼-in. (5 mm) hem. Pin, baste, and machine stitch in place.

6 Each zigzag is 6 in. (15 cm) wide. Divide the width of each finished skirt panel by 6 to work out how many zigzags will run along each side of the dust ruffle. If the width is not exactly divisible by 6, adjust the size of the zigzag until the width of the zigzag divides the width of each panel exactly. Make the template (see Templates, page 177).

7 Take the three pieces of fabric for the skirt and pin the two side panels right sides together.

8 Place the pinned side panels on a flat surface. Measure ⅝ in. (1.5 cm) from the side of the panel (for the seam allowance) and place the template on the panels. Draw around the outline. Continue all the way across the fabric. Finish with a half zigzag and ⅝-in. (1.5 cm) seam allowance. Cut along the marked line and unpin the panels. Repeat for the end panel.

9 Using white thread, overlock the raw edges all along the top and zigzagged bottom of each panel.

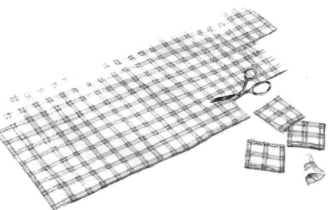

10 Take the check fabric and cut out a series of squares, each 4 x 4 in. (10 x 10 cm). There should be a square for every zigzag along the bottom of the dust ruffle, and half squares for the half zigzags at the corners.

11 Turn each square at an angle so it is diamond shaped. Place one 3 in. (7 cm) above the point of each zigzag. Pin and baste the diamonds in place. Overlock the raw edges of each diamond using thread that matches the main fabric.

12 Join each side panel to the end panel. Pin, baste and machine stitch in place, using a ⅝-in. (1.5 cm) seam allowance. Make sure the zigzags at the end of each panel match perfectly. Press the seams open.

13 Place the skirt on the central panel, right side down, with all raw edges aligned. Match the seams in the skirt panel to the corners of the central panel. Pin, baste, and machine stitch the two together, using a ⅝-in. (1.5 cm) seam allowance.

14 Press the dust ruffle and position it on the bed base.

canopies

Canopies add drama and romance to a bedroom. Even an ordinary divan can be transformed by the addition of flowing drapes. A corona creates a formal, elegant effect, while a simple mosquito net suspended above the bed will add a hint of colonial style. What could be more soothing than drifting off to sleep cocooned in layers of gently flowing fabric?

opposite and below left *A fine organza canopy softens the hard lines of a metal bed. The fabric has been sewn to a hoop that is suspended from the ceiling. A narrow gold velvet ribbon is stitched to the outside edges of the canopy, adding a touch of luxury to a cool white scheme. The crisp white cotton bed linen is edged in matching gold ribbon, unifying the scheme.*

below *A magnificent Shaker cherrywood fourposter is adorned with a panel of bold checks and subtle stripes, loosely knotted to a horizontal support. The practical ties mean that the panel can be easily removed for seasonal changes or laundering.*

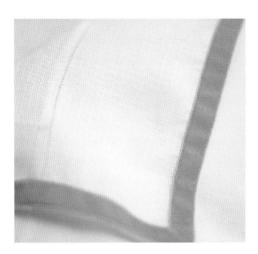

left and far left *A modern metal fourposter with clean minimalist lines is softened with delicate drapery made from hemmed organza and an intricate lace bedspread, which create an ethereal feel without concealing the elegant lines of the bed.*

scalloped corona

A corona brings a regal and elegant air to any bed. The elegant carved-wood corona shown in the picture below is a traditional Swedish design. Similar ready-made coronas can be difficult to find, so here I show how to create the effect using a corona board made from plywood and concealed by a scalloped valance, which adds a majestic finishing touch.

materials & equipment

¾-in. (2 cm) thick plywood for the corona board

angle brackets

flexible curtain track

curtain hooks

woven checked cotton fabric

1-in. (2.5 cm) wide gathering tape

¾-in. (2 cm) wide velcro

tie-on bed curtains

Four-posters are often associated with grand, formal beddressings, but here the austere lines of a very contemporary metal-framed four-poster are softened by eight cotton bed curtains loosely tied to the top of the bed frame. As both sides of the hangings are visible, a woven check fabric has been used to dispense with the need for lining.

materials & equipment

thick Madras cotton check

bias binding in a contrasting color

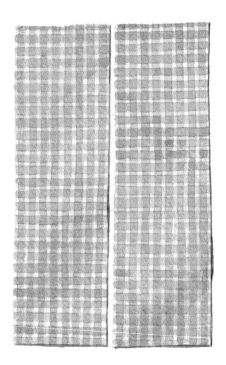

1 To calculate how much material is needed for the eight curtains, measure the bed (see Techniques, page 176). The drop from the top rail of the bed to the floor will give you the length of each curtain. As the curtains are not designed to be drawn, you should only need half a width of 54 in. (135 cm) wide fabric for each one. Cut out the curtains and zigzag the raw edges to prevent fraying.

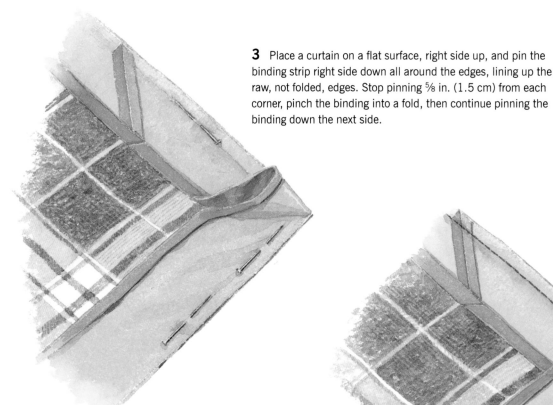

2 You will need enough binding to edge eight curtains and to make 40 ties to hang them with. Make the binding (see Techniques, page 183). Press a ¼-in. (5 mm) fold to the wrong side along one raw edge.

3 Place a curtain on a flat surface, right side up, and pin the binding strip right side down all around the edges, lining up the raw, not folded, edges. Stop pinning ⅝ in. (1.5 cm) from each corner, pinch the binding into a fold, then continue pinning the binding down the next side.

4 Baste and machine stitch the binding in place, ⅝ in. (1.5 cm) from the raw edges. Stitch all the way up to the corner folds, then stop and contine stitching on the other side.

5 When the binding is stitched in place all around the curtain, press the seam flat.

6 Turn the curtain over and fold the pressed edge of the binding to the wrong side of the curtain.

7 Pin and baste the binding in place all around the curtain, folding the corners in as neatly and unobtrusively as you can. Slipstitch to secure.

8 A total of 40 ties are needed, five for each curtain. Cut 40 strips of binding, each 1½ x 16 in. (4 x 40 cm), and make the ties (see Techniques, page 183).

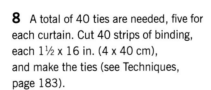

9 Take five ties. Fold them in half and press. Position a tie in each top corner of the curtain and space the others at regular intervals in between. Pin each tie to the back of the binding at the halfway crease. Machine stitch the ties in place.

10 Repeat steps 3 to 9 to make the remaining seven curtains. With loose bows, tie a pair of curtains to each side of the bed frame and a pair at the head and foot of the bed.

pillows

shapes

Mention the words throw pillow and what probably springs to mind is a typical square shape. Although there are some differently shaped pillows available ready-made, if you are prepared to hunt for more unusual pillow forms, or better still, make your own shaped ones by simply stuffing a casing you have sewn yourself, then you can create original pillows in any number of shapes.

this page clockwise from top right A tailored boxed triangle emphasized by thin dark piping; bobble fringe in a deeper contrasting color livens up a plain fabric; a football-shaped pillow with contrasting piping, constructed from four panels, looks ready to fly through the air; green plaid squares echo the square shape of this pillow, which has Turkish corners caught together with a darker green thin piping; a narrow bolster in a woven linen check; a heart outlined with a heavy chenille fringe.
below *Box cubes made from brushed cotton look fun in a modern room.*
bottom A woven checked linen and viscose fabric with a tightly gathered little ruffled edge.
opposite *A mattress effect is created by deep buttoning right through to the back. Great for benches and hard stools.*
opposite below left *A rectangle of horizontal stripes in cotton outlined with a bottle-green wool bobble fringe.*
opposite below right Star struck: this three-dimensional shape can provide the only pattern on a plain sofa or chair.

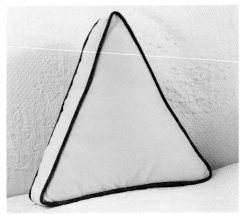

the star

This shape can really provide an unusual accent to
a decorative scheme. It may be tricky to find this shape,
but it is easy to make your own using a satisfyingly simple
mathematical process. This one is made from cotton check
with an embroidered floral motif and is thinly piped
in a contrasting color.

materials & equipment

1³/₄ yd. (120 cm) checked cotton, 44 in. (115 cm) wide

contrasting fabric to make 2³/₄ yd. (2.5 m) of piping

2³/₄ yd. (2.5 m) extra thin piping cord, ¹/₈-in. (3 mm) wide

fiberfill or other stuffing

a sheet of paper 24 x 24 in. (60 x 60 cm)

protractor

compass

bobbles in the round

Circular pillow forms are readily available, though they tend to be of the pancake variety. This pill-shaped size can lend itself to both traditional or modern looks. Here creamy dotted swiss looks almost ethereal with the addition of two rows of cotton bobble fringe. This is trickier to make than it looks, so follow the steps carefully.

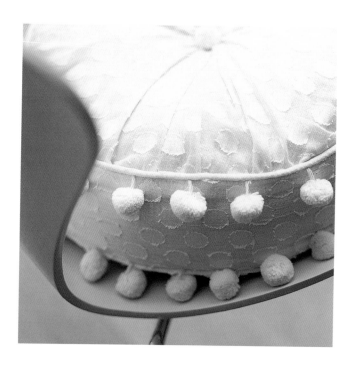

materials & equipment

1¾ yd. (1.6 m) dotted swiss fabric, 60 in. (150 cm) wide

2¾ yd. (2.5 m) piping cord

2¾ yd. (2.5 m) ball fringe

15-in. (38 cm) round pillow form, 4 in. (10 cm) deep

contrasting-color basting thread

1 For the top and bottom of the pillow, cut out two circles of fabric, each with an 18-in. (45 cm) diameter. For the side panel cut out a strip measuring 5 x 49 in. (13 x 123 cm).

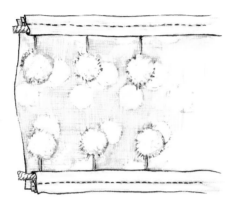

2 Place the side strip right side up. Cut the length of fringe in half and pin and baste a length of bobble fringe along each of the outside edges of the side strip, matching the raw edges.

3 Next make the piping by cutting out the two lengths of fabric on the bias (see Techniques, page 184), each measuring 1 x 49 in. (2½ x 123 cm). Make two lengths of piping (see Techniques, page 185).

4 Lay the piping over the bobble fringe so that the raw edges of the piping point away from the balls, which should lie toward the middle of the side strip. Pin, baste, and machine stitch through all three layers. Repeat for the other long edge of the side strip.

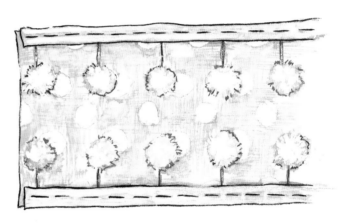

5 To join the ends of the side strip, place the short ends right sides together and machine stitch with a ½-in. (1 cm) seam allowance. Press the seam open. This completes the circular border.

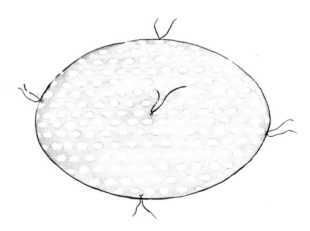

6 For the main body of the pillow, fold each circle of fabric into quarters; mark the center point and each quarter point with a contrasting-colored stitch, on both the perimeters. Use the stitched markers around the two perimeters to mark quarter points on both the top and bottom edges of the circular border.

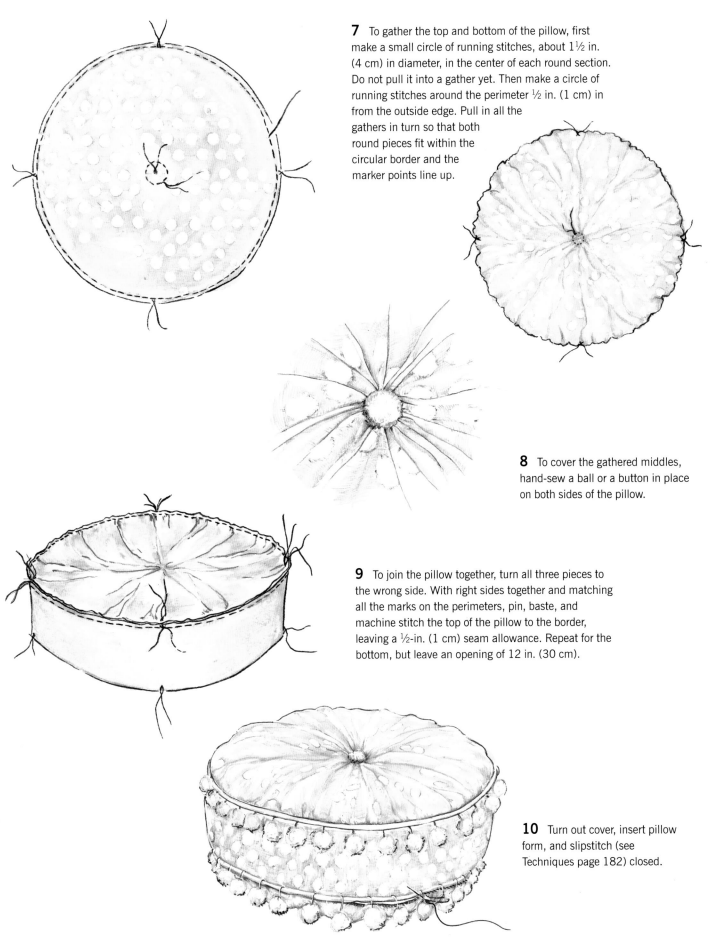

7 To gather the top and bottom of the pillow, first make a small circle of running stitches, about 1½ in. (4 cm) in diameter, in the center of each round section. Do not pull it into a gather yet. Then make a circle of running stitches around the perimeter ½ in. (1 cm) in from the outside edge. Pull in all the gathers in turn so that both round pieces fit within the circular border and the marker points line up.

8 To cover the gathered middles, hand-sew a ball or a button in place on both sides of the pillow.

9 To join the pillow together, turn all three pieces to the wrong side. With right sides together and matching all the marks on the perimeters, pin, baste, and machine stitch the top of the pillow to the border, leaving a ½-in. (1 cm) seam allowance. Repeat for the bottom, but leave an opening of 12 in. (30 cm).

10 Turn out cover, insert pillow form, and slipstitch (see Techniques page 182) closed.

use of fabrics

Fabric is available in a bewildering array. However, if you think beyond the three basic elements of any fabric—color, pattern, and texture—you will see that there are all sorts of ways you can play with these elements for decorative effect. By piecing together clever contrasts and combinations of fabrics, you can achieve spectacular results.

clockwise from top right *An exquisitely delicate cut velvet and chenille tassel dangles on the corner of a woven organdy ribbon pillow; the regal-looking crest on this impressive pillow is sewn directly onto the front and is set off by the rich gold metallic piping with looped corners; rich woven damask needs only the adornment of a thin rope border; a cotton and gaufraged velvet stripe looks smart with chenille fringing; the pattern of this fabric emphasizes the long bolster shape; a white wool bobble fringe trims a strong animal-skin print.*

below *Gaufraged golden thistles on wine-colored velvet, edged in two-tone rope and tassels.*

bottom *Jewel colored wool and mohair to keep you warm.*

opposite above right *A patchwork of rich and sumptuous silks, separated by a golden metallic ribbon, edged in a multicolored tasseled fringe.*

opposite above far right *This lovely antique needlepoint pillow is trimmed with golden ribbon and a tassled fringe.*

opposite *A harlequin velvet pillow and a knife-edged golden cotton damask one.*

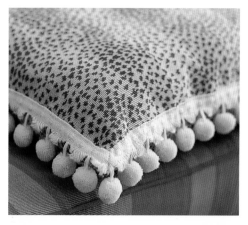

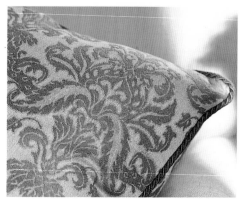

stripes into squares

A pillow to add a touch of imperial style to a daybed
or sofa. Link the material and tassel to other color themes
in the room, or perhaps let it stand alone to make
a bold statement in what might otherwise be a drab corner.
Here, construction and design rely on four triangles mitered
together into a square.

materials & equipment

1½ yd. (1.35 m) striped cotton, 4 in. (115 cm) wide

¾ yd. (70 cm) thick piping cord for ties

decorative tassel

18-in. (45 cm) square pillow form

1 For the front of the pillow, cut four pieces of fabric into identical triangles, each 18½ x 13¼ x 13¼ in. (47 x 12.75 x 12.75 cm), which includes a ½-in. (1 cm) seam allowance.

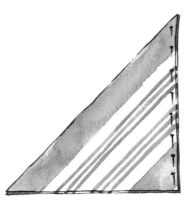

2 Place two of the triangles right sides together. Carefully align the stripes and pin, baste, and machine-stitch along a ½-in. (1 cm) seam. Repeat for the other two triangles. Open out and press the seams open.

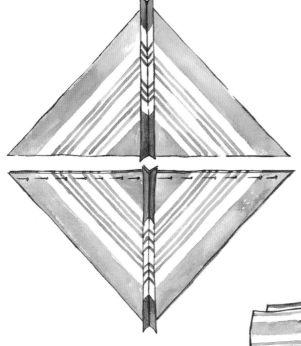

3 Place the two seamed triangles right sides together. Carefully align the stripes, and pin, baste, and machine stitch together along the straight edge. Press open the seam.

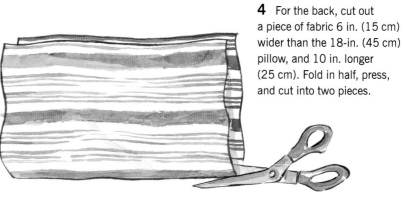

4 For the back, cut out a piece of fabric 6 in. (15 cm) wider than the 18-in. (45 cm) pillow, and 10 in. longer (25 cm). Fold in half, press, and cut into two pieces.

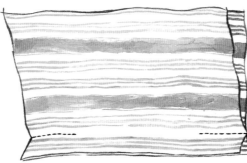

5 Lay the two pieces right sides together. Pin, baste, and machine-stitch a seam along one of the long sides 2 in. (5 cm) from the edge, leaving a 14-in. (35 cm) gap in the middle. Press open.

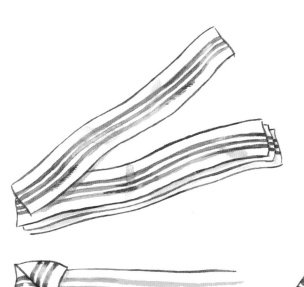

6 Cut out four rectangular strips of striped fabric, each 3 x 23 in. (8 x 58 cm). Position the stripes lengthwise down each of the strips, centered on the width.

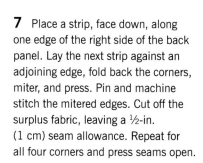

7 Place a strip, face down, along one edge of the right side of the back panel. Lay the next strip against an adjoining edge, fold back the corners, miter, and press. Pin and machine stitch the mitered edges. Cut off the surplus fabric, leaving a ½-in. (1 cm) seam allowance. Repeat for all four corners and press seams open.

8 Lay the mitered border wrong side up over the right side of the back panel. Pin and machine-stitch along the outer edge, leaving a ½-in. (1 cm) seam allowance. Turn the border right side out and press.

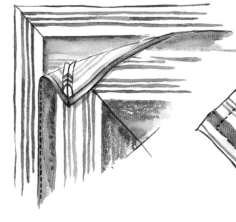

9 Turn the work over so that the border is right side up. Lay the front panel right side up to fit inside the border. Turn all the edges of the front panel under by ½ in. (1 cm) and pin 2 in. (5 cm) from the inside edge of the border. Machine-stitch very carefully along the edge, taking in the border fabric and the back panel. Press.

10 To fasten the back opening, cut out four squares of the fabric, each ¾ in. (1.5 cm) square. Turn under ¼ in. (5 mm) all around. Press and machine-stitch directly onto the back flaps, leaving a small opening to insert the piping cord. Machine-stitch over the opening and knot the ends of the cord. Sew the tassel onto the front.

ribbon weave

This sumptuous woven ribbon pillow works on the simple principle of basket weaving. Seven different shades of velvet ribbon are cut into strips of equal length and woven across the surface of the pillow. This idea can be adapted using just two or three colors for a checkerboard effect or even just one color to show off the weave.

materials & equipment

⅝ yd. (50 cm) thin interlining fabric

⅝ yd. (50 cm) velvet fabric, 44 in. (115 cm) wide

seven different colors of velvet ribbon, 1 in. wide, with a total length of 21 yd. (19 m)

2¼ yd. (2 m) velvet cording

four tassels

18-in. (45 cm) zipper

18-in. (45 cm) square pillow form

1 To create the ribbon effect on the front, cut 19-in. (48 cm) strips from each color of ribbon. It does not matter if there are more strips of some colors—this will add to the effect. Cut out a piece of interlining fabric 19 in. (48 cm) square.

2 Pin the strips face up along one edge of the interlining, leaving a ½-in. (1 cm) gap on each of the sides. Try to achieve a random effect when positioning the colors. Baste and machine stitch along the top of the ribbons to secure them, using a ½-in. seam allowance.

3 Starting from the top, weave the remaining ribbons horizontally, threading them under and over the vertical ribbons. Alternate the colors to create a random pattern and anchor them at the sides with pins. Push each ribbon tightly against the one above.

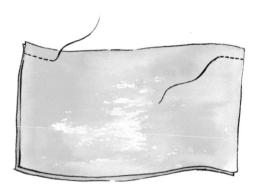

4 Continue weaving the ribbons until the interlining is covered, and then baste the three loose sides down.

5 For the back, cut out two pieces of velvet measuring 10½ x 19 in. (26 x 48 cm). Place the panels right sides together, and along one of the longer sides, machine stitch in from the edge for 2 in. (5 cm) on each side; use a seam allowance of 1½ in. (2 cm). Open the seams out and press.

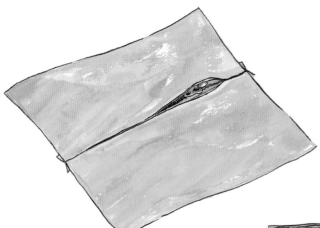

6 Lay the closed zipper underneath the opening, right side up and between the two seams, making sure that the fabric actually meets over the middle of the zipper. Pin, baste, and machine stitch down both sides of the zipper to secure it in place.

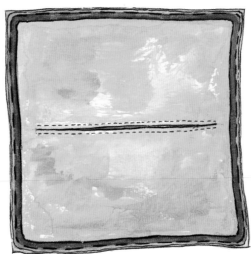

7 Lay the velvet cording around the edge of the back piece on the right side, lining up the raw edges. Pin and baste together.

8 With right sides together, position the front section over the corded back panel, making sure the zipper is open. Pin, baste, and machine stitch through all the layers as close to the cording as possible. Clip the corners, and trim and finish the raw edges to prevent fraying.

9 Turn the cover right side out, insert the pillow form, and close the zipper. Attach a tassel to each corner with small hand stitches.

trimmings and fastenings

Unadorned, a pillow tends to blend into the seating or surface it is placed upon. To make a feature of the pillow itself calls for some clever ideas to dress up the basic shape. Choose from the wealth of decorative trimmings and fastenings available to embellish pillows in dozens of ways.

below *Three examples of back fastening ties: finished with knots; secured by square tabs of the fabric; doubled cotton with zigzagged edges.*

below left *Three rows of a deep natural cotton fringe cover the surface of cream cotton to make a funky pillow.*

bottom left *A striped silk pillow has a doubled ruffled edge, finished with a pleated satin ribbon.*

bottom right *For a neat finish on this plaid pillow, the fan edging has been box-pleated at each of the corners.*

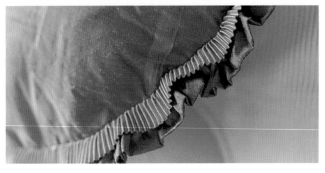

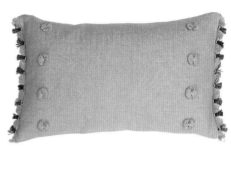

above left and right *Two rectangles: one has a thick fringe to contrast with the subtle plaid, the other is finished in a two-tone fan edging with four tufted linen buttons sewn down each side.*

above center *A finely woven pure white linen pillow has a surface-applied fringe made of natural hemp like string.*

clockwise from top right *Buttons and tufts: silk looped button; deep tufted linen; a wonderful antique handsewn button; a tuft made from cutting a square piece of fabric with pinking shears. The diamond shape and the circular patchwork detail are outlined by rows of tiny bobble fringe in a dark purple. A crewelwork pillow is trimmed in dark green linen fringe.*

rope-edged knotted cushion

A cool Indian madras cotton is paired with
a bright red rope border, sewn directly onto
the edge of the pillow. The extended corners are long
enough to be knotted, for a fresh and different look.
A pile of pillows in inexpensive contrasting fabrics
can look gloriously exuberant.

materials & equipment

2¼ yd. (2 m) cotton fabric, 44 in. (115 cm) wide

5½ yd. (5 m) rope edging

18-in. (45 cm) square pillow form

40-in. (1 m) square piece of pattern paper

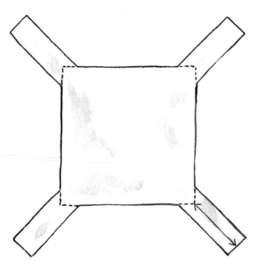

1 Make a paper pattern in the shape of the template shown; the main panel of the pillow measures 19 in. (48 cm) square, and at each corner there is an extension or "tail" 10 in. (25 cm) long and 3 in. (8 cm) wide.

2 Fold the fabric in half, right sides together, matching raw edges. Place the paper pattern on the fabric and pin it in place. Cut out two pieces.

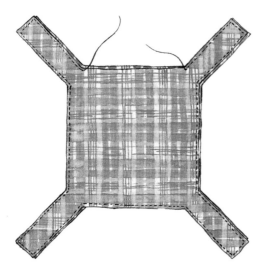

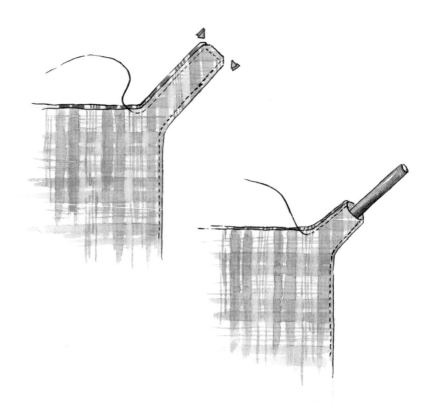

3 Remove the paper pattern and pin, baste, and machine-stitch all around the edge of the panel and the tails using a ½-in. (1 cm) seam allowance. Leave one side of the panel open to insert the pillow. Trim the corners and turn the tails inside out as you sew, pushing out the corners with the blunt end of a pencil or a knitting needle.

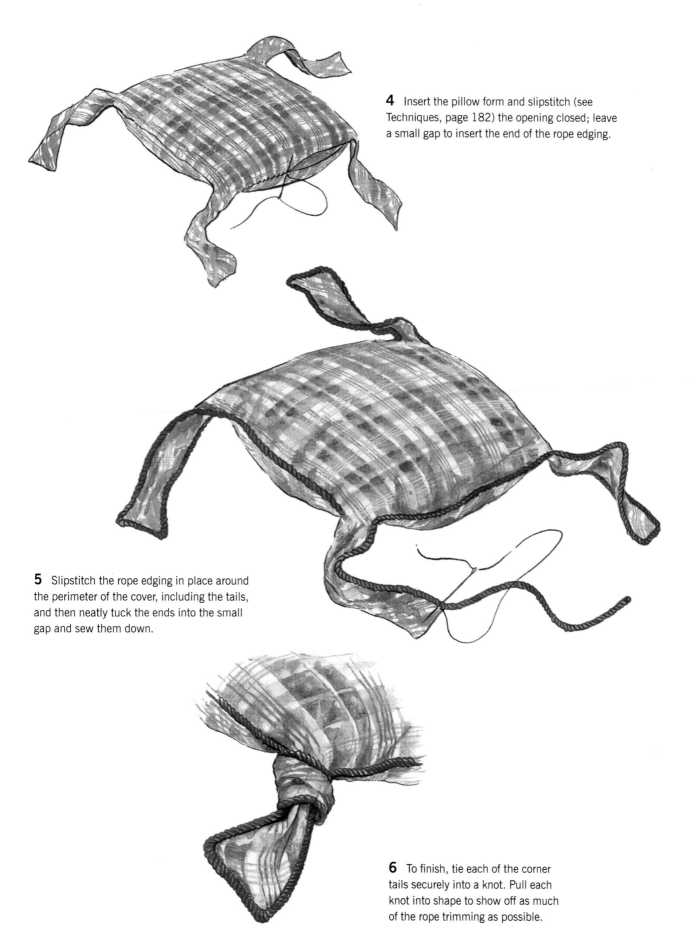

4 Insert the pillow form and slipstitch (see Techniques, page 182) the opening closed; leave a small gap to insert the end of the rope edging.

5 Slipstitch the rope edging in place around the perimeter of the cover, including the tails, and then neatly tuck the ends into the small gap and sew them down.

6 To finish, tie each of the corner tails securely into a knot. Pull each knot into shape to show off as much of the rope trimming as possible.

fastened with tassels

In this formal design, pure white linen encases a silk inner lining to create a sleek and sophisticated pillow. These luxurious fabrics are appropriately dressed up with a pair of silk tassels that provide an elegant means of fastening, and the open end of the linen casing is delicately edged with drawn-thread embroidery.

materials & equipment

⅝ yd. (50 cm) cream evenweave linen, 44 in. (115 cm) wide

1 yd. (90 cm) striped silk, 44 in. (115 cm) wide

two silk tassels

16-in. (40 cm) square pillow form

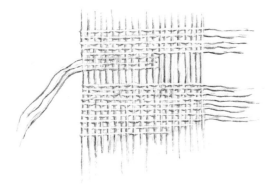

1 For the outer casing, cut out one piece of linen fabric measuring 19 x 37 in. (47 x 92 cm). To decorate the top border, make a line of drawn thread work. Begin by drawing out five threads, 3 in. (8 cm) from one of the longer sides.

2 On the same long edge, turn under a 1-in. (2.5 cm) double hem. Neatly align the folded edge close to the line of drawn threads and press. Baste this fold down.

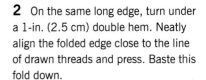

3 Secure your thread at one end of the hem, then pass the needle under three threads, pulling them into a bundle. Sew a small vertical stitch through the right side, coming out through the turned hem, to the right of the thread bundle. Continue this pattern for the length of the hem.

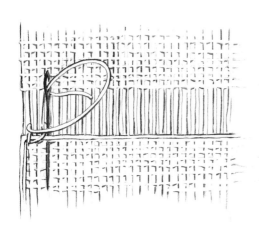

4 Turn the fabric upside down and repeat this stitching on the opposite edge, working from left to right and taking the same threads in each bundle as those taken opposite. The result will be a ladder pattern.

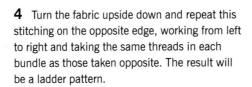

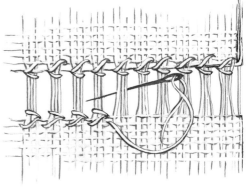

5 Make the casing by folding it in half across the width, right sides together, and lining up the edges. Pin, baste, and machine stitch around the two undecorated sides, using a ½-in. (1 cm) seam allowance.

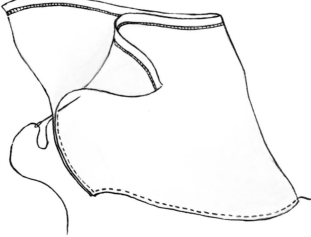

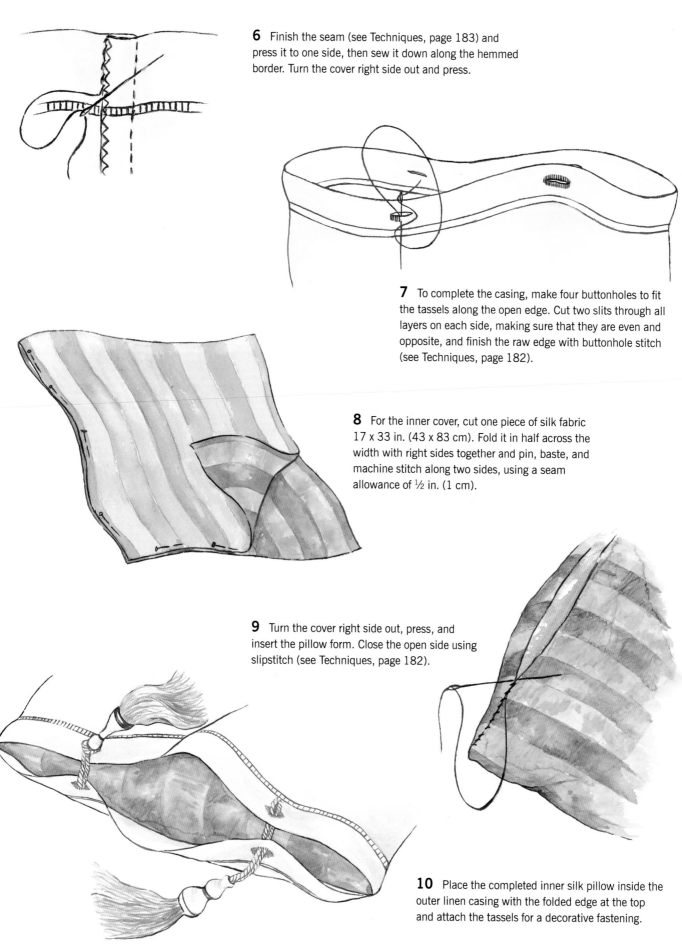

6 Finish the seam (see Techniques, page 183) and press it to one side, then sew it down along the hemmed border. Turn the cover right side out and press.

7 To complete the casing, make four buttonholes to fit the tassels along the open edge. Cut two slits through all layers on each side, making sure that they are even and opposite, and finish the raw edge with buttonhole stitch (see Techniques, page 182).

8 For the inner cover, cut one piece of silk fabric 17 x 33 in. (43 x 83 cm). Fold it in half across the width with right sides together and pin, baste, and machine stitch along two sides, using a seam allowance of ½ in. (1 cm).

9 Turn the cover right side out, press, and insert the pillow form. Close the open side using slipstitch (see Techniques, page 182).

10 Place the completed inner silk pillow inside the outer linen casing with the folded edge at the top and attach the tassels for a decorative fastening.

loose linen cover

Two squares of cool striped beige linen with pairs
of ties on each side cover an inner pillow of
contrasting striped fabric. A simple-to-make pillow
that will make a big impact, this idea is excellent for
giving a quick facelift to older pillows that are
looking a little "tired."

materials & equipment

²/₃ yd. (60 cm) beige striped linen fabric, 44 in. (115 cm) wide

⁵/₈ yd. (50 cm) red striped cotton fabric, 44 in. (115 cm) wide

*5³/₈ yd. (5 m) webbing or cotton tape in brown,
1 in. (1.5 cm) wide*

5³/₈ yd. (5 m) webbing or cotton tape in cream, ½ in. (1.5 cm) wide

18-in. (45 cm) square pillow form

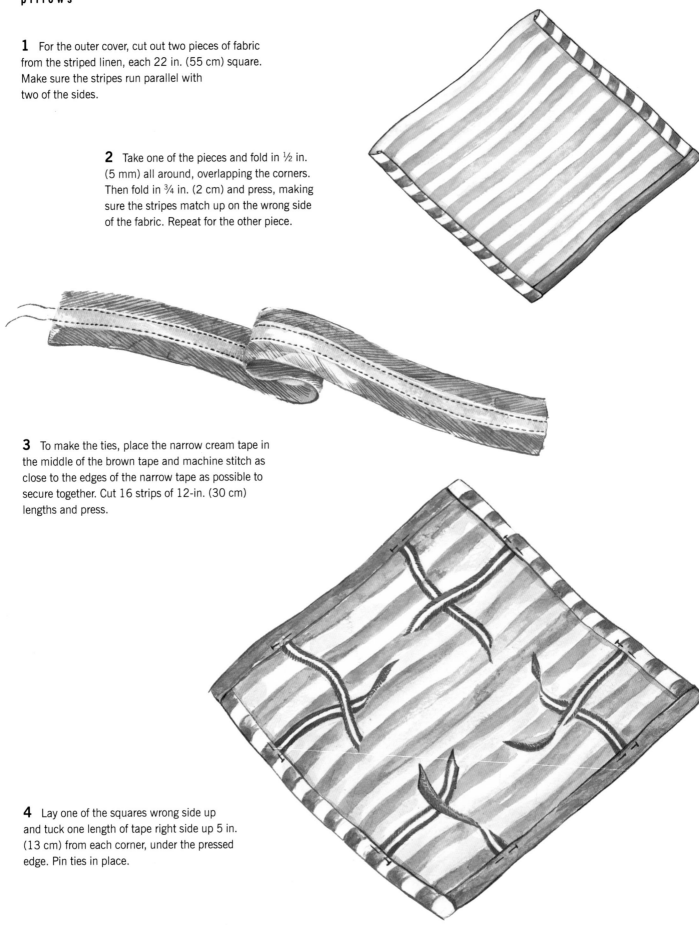

1 For the outer cover, cut out two pieces of fabric from the striped linen, each 22 in. (55 cm) square. Make sure the stripes run parallel with two of the sides.

2 Take one of the pieces and fold in ½ in. (5 mm) all around, overlapping the corners. Then fold in ¾ in. (2 cm) and press, making sure the stripes match up on the wrong side of the fabric. Repeat for the other piece.

3 To make the ties, place the narrow cream tape in the middle of the brown tape and machine stitch as close to the edges of the narrow tape as possible to secure together. Cut 16 strips of 12-in. (30 cm) lengths and press.

4 Lay one of the squares wrong side up and tuck one length of tape right side up 5 in. (13 cm) from each corner, under the pressed edge. Pin ties in place.

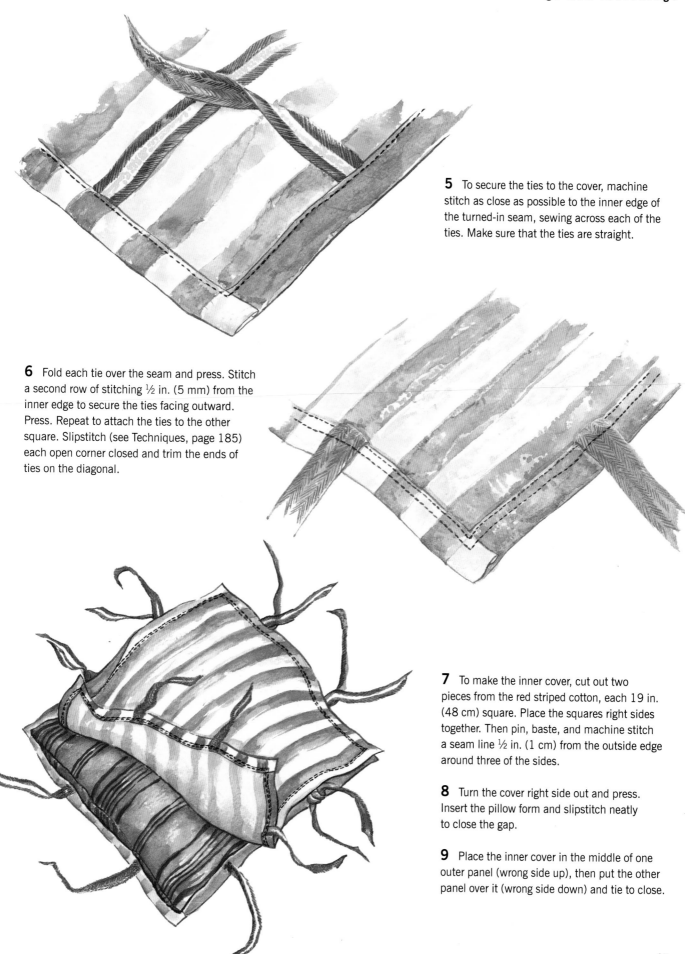

5 To secure the ties to the cover, machine stitch as close as possible to the inner edge of the turned-in seam, sewing across each of the ties. Make sure that the ties are straight.

6 Fold each tie over the seam and press. Stitch a second row of stitching ½ in. (5 mm) from the inner edge to secure the ties facing outward. Press. Repeat to attach the ties to the other square. Slipstitch (see Techniques, page 185) each open corner closed and trim the ends of ties on the diagonal.

7 To make the inner cover, cut out two pieces from the red striped cotton, each 19 in. (48 cm) square. Place the squares right sides together. Then pin, baste, and machine stitch a seam line ½ in. (1 cm) from the outside edge around three of the sides.

8 Turn the cover right side out and press. Insert the pillow form and slipstitch neatly to close the gap.

9 Place the inner cover in the middle of one outer panel (wrong side up), then put the other panel over it (wrong side down) and tie to close.

surface decoration

For those who want to be challenged beyond running up pillows or covers on a sewing machine—or indeed for those who enjoy the slower pace of stitching by hand —there are numerous ways of applying surface decoration to your own or ready-made pillows. Cross stitch, embroidery, quilting, and appliqué can all be used to add decorative and personal touches.

far left *Hand stitched parallel rows of white knitting wool yarn create a fine pattern on black wool.*

left *Black on white felt—painstakingly ordered circles have been cut out to provide the pattern on this white inner pillow.*

below left *Cream linen has been bordered in cross-stitched black embroidery thread; the back of the pillow is a black-and-white checked gingham.*

below *A brown boiled wool pillow has been embroidered with charming naive multicolored flowers and finished with thick red rope.*

bottom *A corner detail of a wool and velvet ribbon patchwork pillow.*

  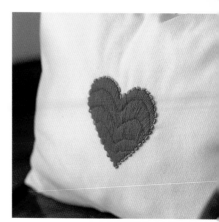

left *Embroidered leopard-skin tapestry looks like the real thing!*

below from left to right *Strong yellow ovals of wool in satin stitch outlined in black. The most delicate flowers are intricately stitched onto cream linen. Leftover fabrics and a carefully cut initial appliquéd together.*

bottom from left to right *Hand-painted silk makes an elegant pillow. The brown knitted pillow has been tie-dyed and felted to give a unique finish, while the top pillow is a patchwork of velvet ribbon, knitted wool squares, and woven linen. A satin-stitch embroidered heart in thick yarn on fine cream flannel.*

autumnal appliqué

Like many other forms of needlecraft, appliqué has survived for generations and lends itself to all manner of designs, pictorial or abstract. All you need to do is decide on a motif, or series of motifs, draw and cut them out from scraps of fabric, and apply them to a background. There is a template for the leaves on page 177.

materials & equipment

⁵⁄₈ yd. (50 cm) heavy cotton fabric, 44 in. (115 cm) wide

¼ yd. (25 cm) contrasting fabric for the motif, 44 in. (115 cm) wide

¼ yd. (25 cm) fusible bonding web, 20 in. (50 cm) wide

18-in. (45 cm) square pillow form

tracing paper

1 Cut out two pieces of the heavy cotton fabric, each measuring 19 x 19 in. (47 x 47 cm), for the front and back panels. Make sure the grain of the fabric is straight, not diagonal.

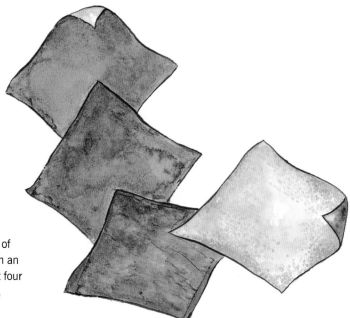

2 Place the fusible web on the wrong side of the piece of contrasting fabric and bond with an iron, following package instructions. Cut out four squares to fit the leaf motifs (see Templates, page 177).

3 Draw the shapes of the appliqué leaf motifs on the tracing paper, increasing the proportions to the desired size. Cut them out, and lay them over the contrasting fabric squares. Secure them in place with pins and carefully cut out each leaf.

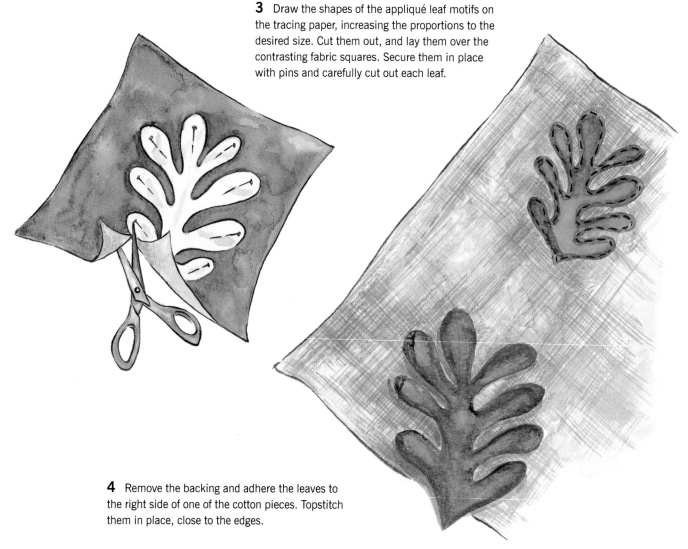

4 Remove the backing and adhere the leaves to the right side of one of the cotton pieces. Topstitch them in place, close to the edges.

5 To decorate the leaves, machine stitch the outline of the veins and the stalks in a different colored thread using a tight zigzag stitch.

6 To assemble the cover, lay the remaining piece of cotton over the appliquéd piece, with right sides together. Pin, baste, and machine stitch along three sides, using a seam allowance of ½ in. (1 cm).

7 Turn right side out, insert the pillow form, and slipstitch (see Techniques, page 182) the open end closed.

lampshades

shapes

Lampshades come in all manner of shapes, and the outline of the basic frame is what gives the shade its intrinsic character. There are plenty of shapes to choose from, including drums and cylinders; cones of all sorts, from the more open Empire and coolie to the tall narrow chimney; bowed shades with a concave profile; or more solid-looking straight-sided shades, which may be hexagonal or boxlike, in the form of a gently tapering square or rectangle.

clockwise from below far left
Pale cream and neutral colors in plain silk show off stylish shapes: a three-dimensional pinch-pleated ruffle border sits on the widely flaring rim of a bowed oval shade, emphasizing the exaggerated curve; gathered silk covers a basic square frame; a waisted square, bordered in a darker contrasting trim; a six-panelled hexagonal star frame; neat gathers caught in a collar; an unusual bell shape, completely covered in at the top; tapering sides and a neat band at the base lift a square frame.

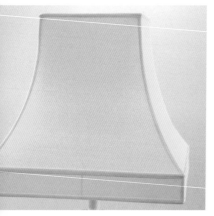
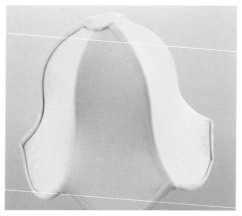

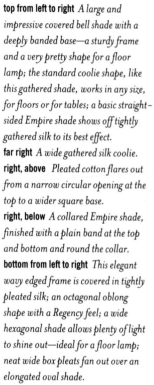

top from left to right *A large and impressive covered bell shade with a deeply banded base—a sturdy frame and a very pretty shape for a floor lamp; the standard coolie shape, like this gathered shade, works in any size, for floors or for tables; a basic straight-sided Empire shade shows off tightly gathered silk to its best effect.*

far right *A wide gathered silk coolie.*

right, above *Pleated cotton flares out from a narrow circular opening at the top to a wider square base.*

right, below *A collared Empire shade, finished with a plain band at the top and bottom and round the collar.*

bottom from left to right *This elegant wavy edged frame is covered in tightly pleated silk; an octagonal oblong shape with a Regency feel; a wide hexagonal shade allows plenty of light to shine out—ideal for a floor lamp; neat wide box pleats fan out over an elongated oval shade.*

pleated coolie

A buttery yellow silk taffeta is tightly pleated all around the top
of this small coolie, and the pleats fan out evenly around the
gently flaring sides for a crisp clean effect. The lamp is then
given a punchy finish with scarlet trimming around the top and
bottom rings. The inner silk lining protects the outer cover and
gives the whole design a highly professional finish.

materials & equipment

*coolie frame with six struts and base gimbal fixture 4 in. (10 cm)
diameter top; 10 in. (25 cm) diameter bottom; 5 in. (13 cm) height*

20 in. (50 cm) silk lining, 45 in. (115 cm) wide

10 in. (25 cm) butter-yellow silk taffeta, 60 in. (150 cm) wide

3 x 37 in. (8 x 92 cm) strip of red silk taffeta

½ in. (1 cm) wide binding tape

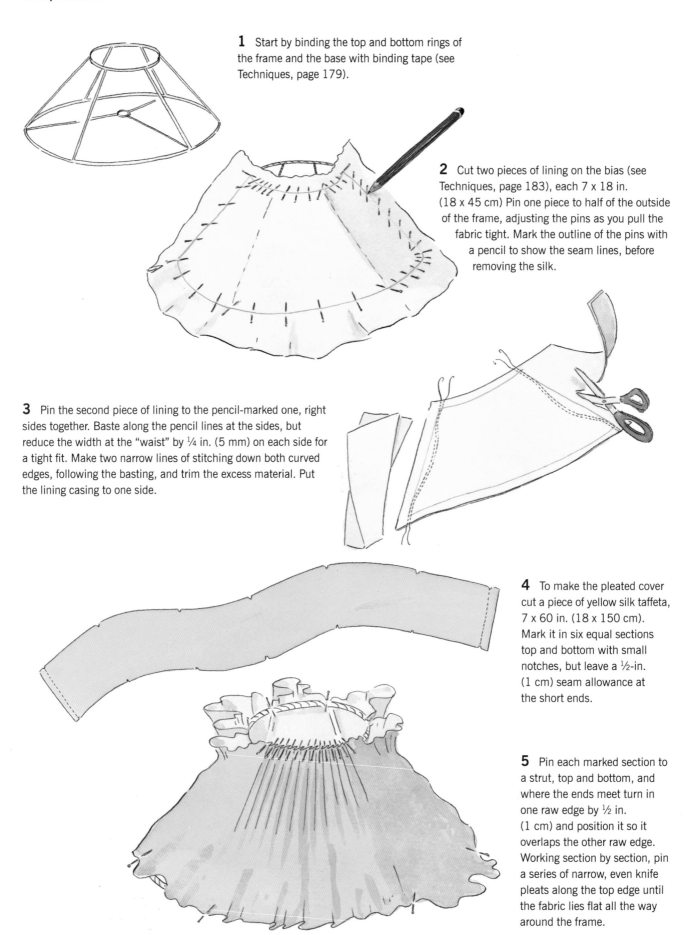

1 Start by binding the top and bottom rings of the frame and the base with binding tape (see Techniques, page 179).

2 Cut two pieces of lining on the bias (see Techniques, page 183), each 7 x 18 in. (18 x 45 cm) Pin one piece to half of the outside of the frame, adjusting the pins as you pull the fabric tight. Mark the outline of the pins with a pencil to show the seam lines, before removing the silk.

3 Pin the second piece of lining to the pencil-marked one, right sides together. Baste along the pencil lines at the sides, but reduce the width at the "waist" by ¼ in. (5 mm) on each side for a tight fit. Make two narrow lines of stitching down both curved edges, following the basting, and trim the excess material. Put the lining casing to one side.

4 To make the pleated cover cut a piece of yellow silk taffeta, 7 x 60 in. (18 x 150 cm). Mark it in six equal sections top and bottom with small notches, but leave a ½-in. (1 cm) seam allowance at the short ends.

5 Pin each marked section to a strut, top and bottom, and where the ends meet turn in one raw edge by ½ in. (1 cm) and position it so it overlaps the other raw edge. Working section by section, pin a series of narrow, even knife pleats along the top edge until the fabric lies flat all the way around the frame.

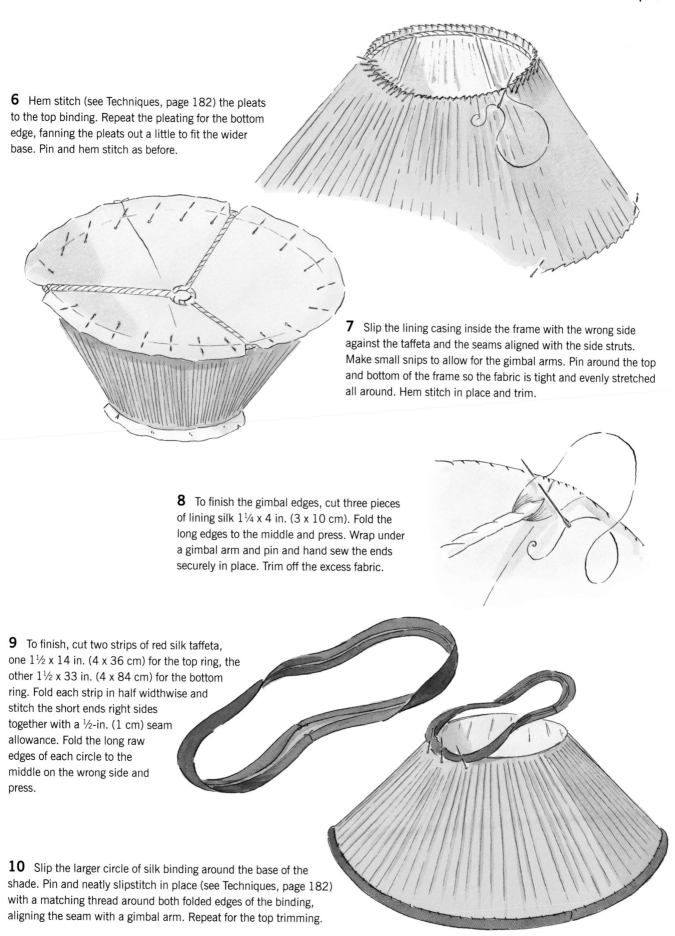

6 Hem stitch (see Techniques, page 182) the pleats to the top binding. Repeat the pleating for the bottom edge, fanning the pleats out a little to fit the wider base. Pin and hem stitch as before.

7 Slip the lining casing inside the frame with the wrong side against the taffeta and the seams aligned with the side struts. Make small snips to allow for the gimbal arms. Pin around the top and bottom of the frame so the fabric is tight and evenly stretched all around. Hem stitch in place and trim.

8 To finish the gimbal edges, cut three pieces of lining silk 1¼ x 4 in. (3 x 10 cm). Fold the long edges to the middle and press. Wrap under a gimbal arm and pin and hand sew the ends securely in place. Trim off the excess fabric.

9 To finish, cut two strips of red silk taffeta, one 1½ x 14 in. (4 x 36 cm) for the top ring, the other 1½ x 33 in. (4 x 84 cm) for the bottom ring. Fold each strip in half widthwise and stitch the short ends right sides together with a ½-in. (1 cm) seam allowance. Fold the long raw edges of each circle to the middle on the wrong side and press.

10 Slip the larger circle of silk binding around the base of the shade. Pin and neatly slipstitch in place (see Techniques, page 182) with a matching thread around both folded edges of the binding, aligning the seam with a gimbal arm. Repeat for the top trimming.

use of fabrics and trimmings

Second only to the shape of the lampshade, the type of fabric and trimming you choose to cover the frame will dictate the overall look of the shade. For instance, the same basic cone would look very different covered in a laminated striped cloth than if you decided on a loose, skirtlike cover in a floral print. Both heavy-and lightweight fabrics alike can be used to decorate lampshades.

far left *A small coolie-shaped top is edged in a deep band, covered by neat knife pleats of cream silk and lengthened by a silk fringe.*
left, above *A lightweight cotton fabric has been dipped in fabric stiffener and then diagonally draped over an Empire shade for a sumptuous ruched effect.*
left, below *The finest ecru silk is tightly gathered around a coolie shade and finished with a pinked skirt.*
bottom from left *Cotton ticking stripes meet perfectly across the angles of this panelled shade to form a chevron design; a regal red crushed velvet is stiffened with lamination and trimmed with leather; moiré silk in contrasting colors complements the shaped panels of this stylish shade.*

right *Delicate cream lace is generously gathered and held in place over a plain cream shade by a pretty satin ribbon tied in a bow.*

far right *A crisp red-and-white cotton gingham is shown to best effect on a simple Empire shape. The geometric check accentuates the perfect knife pleats, which are finished in a binding of the same checked fabric, used on the diagaonal.*

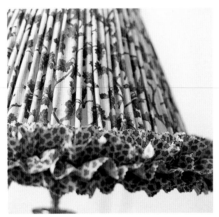

above from left *Double pinked ruffles in a complementary fabric with a smaller motif edge this tighly gathered printed cotton shade; this unusual shade is created using a thin printed cotton which is stiffened with lamination and then scored into shaped sections—bias binding finishes the raw edges and a ribbon threaded through the scored sections pulls the shade into tight gathers to form a petal pattern along the top edge; a coolie-shaped frame is covered in a tightly gathered printed cotton, and trimmed along the bottom edge in a strongly contrasting deep cotton fringe.*

right *Checked voile is used as a loose cover over a collared Empire silk shade. The delicate fabric stands out stiffly from the smocked top, and the top and bottom edges are finished in red velvet piping.*

skirted pictorial print

Patterned fabrics work as well as plains, particularly on loose fabric lampshades. Here, a pretty red and white *toile de Jouy* is sewn into a full, pleated skirt set off with a bold matching trim that sits on the bottom edge. The shade is given extra fullness with the addition of an underskirt between the outer cover and the lining.

materials & equipment

frame with six struts and reverse gimbal fixture: 7 in. (18 cm) diameter top; 12 in. (30 cm) diameter bottom; 8 in. (20 cm) height

1 ³/₈ yd. (125 cm) lining fabric, 45 in. (115 cm) wide

1 ¹/₄ yd. (100 cm) toile de Jouy fabric, 55 in. (140 cm) wide

1 ¹/₂ yd. (140 cm) coordinating trimming, 1 ¹/₄ in. (3 cm) wide

¹/₂ in. (1 cm) wide binding tape

1 Start by binding the top and bottom rings and the side struts with binding tape (see Techniques, page 179).

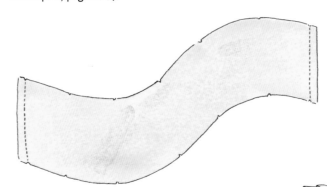

2 Cut out a piece of lining fabric 9 x 39 in. (23 x 98 cm) and mark the long edges into six equal sections by making small notches at the top and bottom, but leaving a ½-in. (1 cm) seam allowance at the two short ends.

3 Pin the fabric to the bottom of the frame matching the notches with the six side struts. Pull the fabric up inside the frame and pin the marked sections to the six side struts at the top; cut two slits to fit the fabric around the gimbal, then pin small, even pleats between the struts. Where the fabric meets, turn under ½ in. (1 cm) on one edge, then place ½ in. (1 cm) of the opposite side under the turned one.

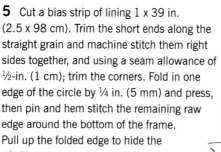

4 Hem stitch (see Techniques, page 182) the lining in place top and bottom.

5 Cut a bias strip of lining 1 x 39 in. (2.5 x 98 cm). Trim the short ends along the straight grain and machine stitch them right sides together, and using a seam allowance of ½-in. (1 cm); trim the corners. Fold in one edge of the circle by ¼ in. (5 mm) and press, then pin and hem stitch the remaining raw edge around the bottom of the frame. Pull up the folded edge to hide the stitches.

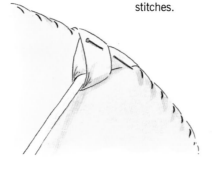

6 Cut out two strips of lining fabric 1½ x 3 in. (4 x 8 cm) Fold both long edges to the middle and wrap under each arm. Pin and neatly handsew the ends to the top of the frame and trim the excess fabric.

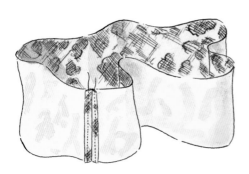

7 Now cut two pieces of *toile de Jouy* fabric and machine stitch them together, using a 1-in. (2.5 cm) seam allowance, to make a strip 11 x 80 in. (28 x 200 cm). Turn under the raw edges on the seam allowance by ¼ in. (5 mm), press and machine down (do not stitch through to the main panel).

8 Turn the bottom edge of the *toile de Jouy* to the right side by ¼ in. (5 mm) and press. Pin, baste, and machine stitch the decorative trim to the right side on the bottom edge, taking in the hem, and hiding all raw edges. Neatly tuck the ends under where they meet.

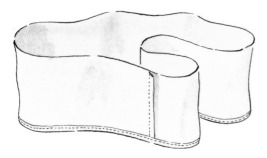

9 To line the skirt, use a piece of lining fabric 11 x 80 in. (28 x 200 cm); join panels where necessary, and the short ends, using a French seam (see Techniques, page 183) with a total allowance of 1 in. (2.5 cm) and press to one side. Turn the bottom edge of the circle to the wrong side making a double ¼-in. (5 mm) hem; pin and machine stitch in place.

10 Place the right side of the lining against the wrong side of the *toile de Jouy*. Pin and baste the raw edges of both layers together ½ in. (1 cm) from the top. Pin and baste a series of pleats about 1 in. (2.5 cm) wide around the top edge. Slip the skirt over the lined shade and pin to the top of the frame; make any necessary adjustments to the pleats to fit the circumference exactly. Hem stitch in place and trim.

11 Cut a strip of *toile de Jouy* on the bias 1½ x 24 in. (4 x 60 cm) and machine stitch the short ends together as in step 5. Turn in one edge by ½ in. (1 cm) and press. Pin the remaining raw edge to the frame, right side down and with the binding on the inside; hem stitch in place. Pull the folded edge over the frame to the outside and secure all the way around with slipstitch (see Techniques, page 182).

woven ribbons

This novel shade is covered with a close basketweave of gingham ribbon. You can choose any sort of ribbon or combination of colors to create your own individual woven shade. Adjust your measurements according to the width of the ribbons used and the size of the frame, and follow the simple weaving principle, finishing the top and bottom with a bright contrast trim.

materials & equipment

rectangular frame with long sides and reversible top gimbal: 10 ½ x 5 in. (26 x 13 cm) bottom; 6 ½ x 3 in. (16 x 8 cm) top; with 10-in. (25 cm) long sides and 4-in. (10 cm) measurement across the middle, top, and bottom

15 yd. (14 m) gingham ribbon, 1-in. (2.5 cm) wide

1 ½ yd. (135 cm) contrasting bias binding, ½-in. (1 cm) wide

½-in. (1 cm) wide binding tape

fabric adhesive

1 Begin by binding the top and bottom of the frame and the side struts (see Techniques, page 179).

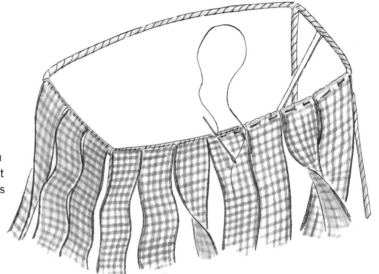

2 For the vertical weave cut out 20 strips of ribbon each measuring 11 in. (28 cm) long. Pin them to the binding at the top of the frame; use seven strips across the long sides and three across the short ends. Space them evenly so they slightly overlap each other. Slipstitch (see Techniques, page 182) the ribbons in place at the top to secure them.

3 Pull each ribbon down and pin to the bottom of the frame. As the bottom is wider than the top, the ribbons will be more spaced out at the base, so make sure this spacing is even. Slipstitch the ribbons to the binding and trim the ends.

4 For the horizontal weave, cut out 10 strips of ribbon each measuring 32 in. (81 cm). Pin each length to one of the side struts, working from the top to the bottom and spacing them evenly. Slipstitch the ribbons in position.

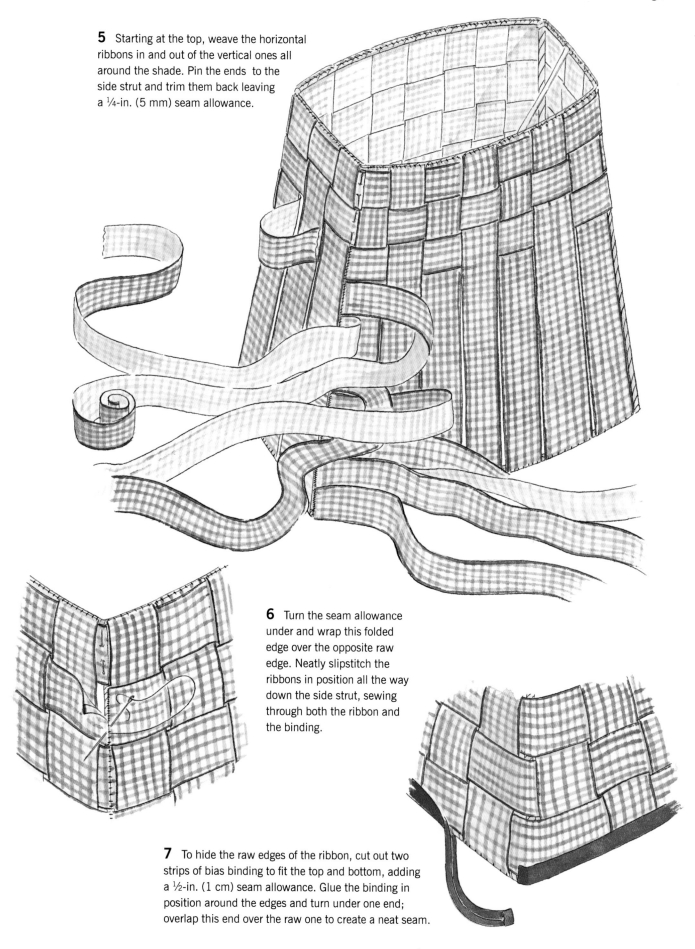

5 Starting at the top, weave the horizontal ribbons in and out of the vertical ones all around the shade. Pin the ends to the side strut and trim them back leaving a ¼-in. (5 mm) seam allowance.

6 Turn the seam allowance under and wrap this folded edge over the opposite raw edge. Neatly slipstitch the ribbons in position all the way down the side strut, sewing through both the ribbon and the binding.

7 To hide the raw edges of the ribbon, cut out two strips of bias binding to fit the top and bottom, adding a ½-in. (1 cm) seam allowance. Glue the binding in position around the edges and turn under one end; overlap this end over the raw one to create a neat seam.

table lamps

The choice of lampshades in this category is overwhelming. Styles include slender candlesticks topped with tiny shades; half shades ideal for setting at each end of a mantelpiece or on a narrow shelf; heavy urnlike bases carrying sizable shades that may sit on a coffee or side table to provide pools of soft, atmospheric light; reading lights set upon a desk; or pretty bedside lamps suitable for the bedroom.

below from left *White-dotted Swiss, finished with a ruffle; a generous Provençal cotton skirt, gathered with a bow; floral cotton, laminated onto a coolie shade and held on a classical glass column base.*

bottom from left *A white plaster base with a cone shade laminated with a bright blue polka dot weave; a tall turned base, topped with a gathered shade in thin blue cotton; this versatile brass table lamp is designed for maximum manoeuvrability and has a precisely pleated shade.*

above *Polka-dotted voile, tightly gathered over this Empire shade, lets out maximum light.*

above left *Pretty and practical: a tilt-top desk lamp with a collared shade is finished in a gathered double ruffle.*

far left *The top and bottom edges of this shade have been smartly finished with pinch-pleated silk and a contrasting color threaded through it.*

left *A gathered coolie with a difference—pale yellow silk is knife pleated and finished in a blue binding, which is picked up by the matching two-toned deep fringe.*

bottom from left *Striped fabric, neatly box pleated over an Empire shade, is finished in a strong complementary bias binding; a narrow tapered oblong is a good shape to use when there is not much space available, such as on a mantelpiece; a traditional double chandelier lamp is updated with a pair of blue-and-white striped gathered shades.*

box-pleated conical shade

Hiding an ordinary conical shade is a box-pleated cover made from a warm red and yellow *toile de Jouy*. The skirt falls in loose, unstructured folds, allowing the pattern of the fabric to remain visible. The bow is a pretty feature, highlighting the waist of the shade and the ruffled effect of the gathered box pleats at the top.

materials & equipment

frame with six struts and reverse gimbal fixture: 5 in. (13 cm) diameter top; 10 in. (25 cm) diameter bottom; 7 in. (18 cm) height

20 in. (50 cm) lining fabric, 45 in. (115 cm) wide

1 ⅝ yd. (150 cm) toile de Jouy fabric, 45 in. (115 cm) wide

½ in. (1 cm) wide binding tape

1 Start by binding the top and bottom rings of the frame and the side struts with binding tape (see Techniques, page 179).

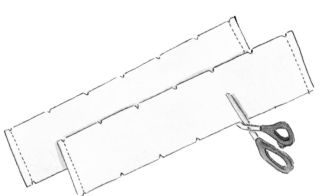

2 Cut two pieces of lining, 8 x 32½ in. (20 x 81 cm) Mark six equal sections on the long edges top and bottom with small notches but leave an extra ½-in. (1 cm) seam allowance at the short ends.

3 Pin one piece of lining fabric to the outside of the frame along the bottom, lining up the notches with the struts. Where the fabric meets, fold back the seam allowance on one end and place it so it overlaps the raw edge on the other side. Pull the fabric up over the frame and start by pinning the notches to the struts, then pin small even pleats between the notches. Hem stitch (see Techniques, page 182) the lining in place and trim.

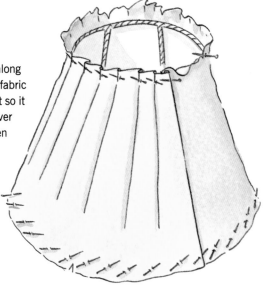

4 Now pin the second piece of lining fabric to the inside of the frame, making two small slits at the top to accommodate the gimbal arms. Line up and pin the fabric as in step 3, but at the top and bottom fold under the edge by ¼-in. (5 mm), positioning it over the existing raw edge for a neat finish. Hem stitch top and bottom and trim.

5 To hide the gimbal arms, cut out two strips of lining fabric 1½ x 3 in. (4 x 7 cm). Fold both the long edges to the middle and wrap each strip under the gimbal arm. Tuck under the raw edge and pin and handsew to the top of the frame.

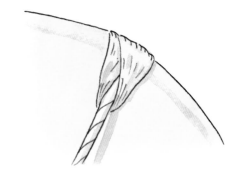

6 For the loose shade, cut out a panel of *toile de Jouy*, 13 x 60 in. (32 x 150 cm), joining pieces and matching the pattern as necessary. Fold the panel in half widthwise, right sides together, and machine stitch the short ends with a ⅝-in. (1.5 cm) seam allowance. To finish the seam, turn each side under by ¼-in. (1.5 cm) and machine stitch down, making sure you do not sew through to the main fabric.

7 Fold in a double ¼-in. (5 mm) hem along the bottom edge of the circle of fabric, pin, baste, and machine stitch. Next fold in the top edge of the fabric to the wrong side by 2½ in. (6.5 cm) and baste in place.

8 Make a series of box pleats around the top by folding the material into itself; there should be 12 pleats, each with two ¾-in. (2 cm) sides and a 1½-in. (4 cm) front panel. Pin the pleats and check the fit on the shade, making small adjustments where necessary. Baste and machine stitch the pleats in place 2 in. (5 cm) below the top edge.

9 Slip the cover over the frame and sew a line of running stitches (see Techniques, page 182) through all layers, just under the top ring and following the stitches made in step 8.

10 To make the bow, cut a 2½ x 55 in. (6.5 x 140 cm) strip of *toile de Jouy*. If necessary, join strips together matching the pattern. Fold in half length-wise with right sides together and cut the short ends at a slight angle. Machine stitch along the long edge and one of the shorter ones using a ¼-in. (5 mm) seam allowance.

11 Use a knitting needle or a safety pin to push the fabric right side out through the open end. Tuck the raw ends to the inside and neatly sew the opening closed. Tie into a bow around the top of the frame.

smocked patterned shade

A pretty blue Provençal skirt with a smocked top is slipped over a plain lined shade; the elasticized top means the cover stays firmly in place. Choose any motif pattern as an alternative. The great thing about this practical design is that it can be removed easily to shake off the dust or for washing.

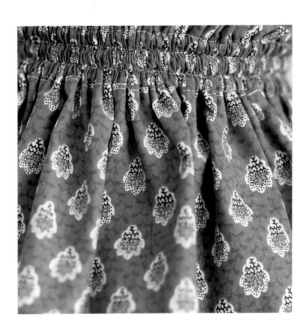

materials & equipment

frame with eight side struts: 6 ½ in. (16 cm) diameter top;
10 in. (25 cm) diameter bottom; 7 in. (18 cm) height, including 1 ½ in. (4 cm) collar

1 ³/₈ yd. (125 cm) lining fabric, 45 in. (115 cm) wide

20 in. (50 cm) Provençal cotton, 60 in. (150 cm) wide

½ in. (1 cm) wide binding tape

1 ⁵/₈ yd. (150 cm) elastic, ¼ in. (5 mm) wide

1 Start by binding all parts of the frame with binding tape (see Techniques, page 179).

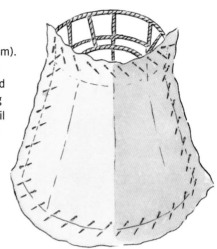

2 Cut four pieces of lining fabric, 8 x 17 in. (20 x 43 cm). Pin one to half of the outside of the frame starting in the middle of the top and bottom rings, then at the sides and corners, and continue pinning at opposite sides, keeping the fabric tight. Mark the outline of the pins with a pencil before removing the lining from the frame. Using this as a template, cut three more pieces of lining fabric, adding a 1 in. (2.5 cm) seam allowance around the pencil outlines.

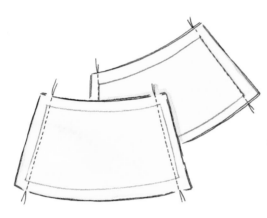

3 For the outer casing, machine stitch two panels of lining fabric together down the sides, right sides facing, and following the pencil lines exactly. Repeat for the inner casing, but reduce the width between the pencil markings by 1/8 in. (3 mm) at each side for a tight fit.

4 Slip the inner casing inside the frame with the wrong side facing out. Line up the side seams with two opposite struts and pin into position around the top and bottom, pulling the fabric tight. Make four small notches at the top to fit the lining around the arms. Hem stitch (see Techniques, page 182) the lining to the binding around the top and bottom of the frame and trim.

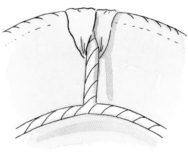

5 Slip the outer lining casing over the top of the shade, aligning the seams with those on the inner casing. Pin and hem stitch in place, top and bottom.

6 Cut out four strips of lining fabric 1 x 2½ in. (2.5 x 6 cm) Fold both long edges to the middle and wrap a strip under each arm of the fixture. Handsew to the frame top and trim.

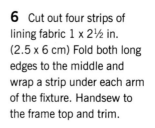

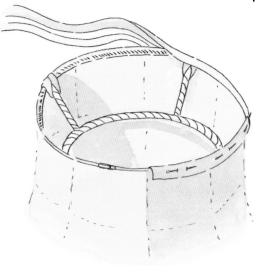

7 To hide the raw edges, cut a strip of lining fabric 1 x 33 in. (2.5 x 82.5 cm) for the bottom and 1 x 22 in. (2.5 x 55 cm) for the top. On both strips fold the long edges to the middle and press. Pin, then slipstitch (see Techniques, page 182) the strips in place along both folded edges, tucking under the raw ends.

8 For the smocked skirt, cut a piece of fabric 18 x 51 in. (45 x 128 cm) Fold it in half, matching the short ends, right sides together and pin and machine stitch, using a ½-in. (1 cm) seam allowance. Press open the seam.

9 With the tube of fabric wrong side out, fold down the top edge by 2½ in. (6 cm) and pin and baste it in place.

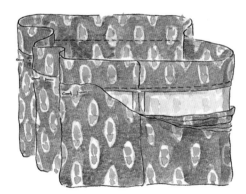

10 Now turn the bottom edge up ¼ in. (5 mm) and press, then fold the whole lower half of the tube upward; overlap the bottom folded edge and the basted raw edge by ¼ in. (5 mm). Pin and machine stitch the overlap, joining all layers.

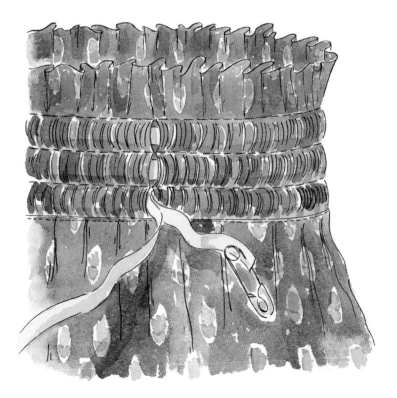

11 Work three parallel lines of stitches ½ in. (1 cm) down from the top edge and ½ in. (1 cm) apart all around the top of the cover. Unpick three holes on the side seam made in step 8. Insert a 19 in. (48 cm) length of elastic into each hole, threading them through with a safety pin. Pull the elastic through and handsew one end over the other with a ½-in. (1 cm) overlap. Slipstitch the openings closed, turn the cover inside out, and fit it over the shade.

wall and ceiling lamps

Ceiling lights tend to operate as main sources of light, often illuminating a whole room. Although they should be capable of casting plenty of light, they should also be a decorative feature and draw the eye up. Wall lights come as uplights, bracket lights, and sconces, and are useful for throwing light onto surrounding surfaces to reflect back into the room.

below from left *Thin yellow cotton was dipped in fabric stiffener and then draped over a panelled shade. The molded shape was then finished with a satin tassel; this fun harlequin chandelier was knitted from fine yellow silk yarn and draped over a ring frame. Gilt coins catch the light and keep the shade in shape; a tightly knitted pagoda-shaped pendant, stretched over a series of ring frames, makes a most effective and clever overhead light fixture.*

right *Thin gray and cream striped voile is tightly gathered to form a dense cover on a circular wall shield, which curves gently to hide the bulb from view on each side. A flame retardant lining is used to prevent scorching.*
far right *A wall sconce throws light in a wide arc up to the ceiling, and creates a wonderfully subtle effect. This one is laminated with rich yellow crushed velvet and edged with a laced leather thong.*

clockwise from top left *A period brass wall bracket with a gathered cotton shade; wall sconces in velvet and pale checked cotton; layered taffeta ribbons finished with beads; yellow laminated hessian on a pendant drum shade; metal eyelets with rings attach a loose shade to a circular frame; pretty printed floaty voile is gathered tightly on a collared pendant.*

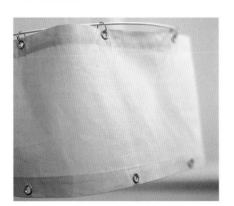

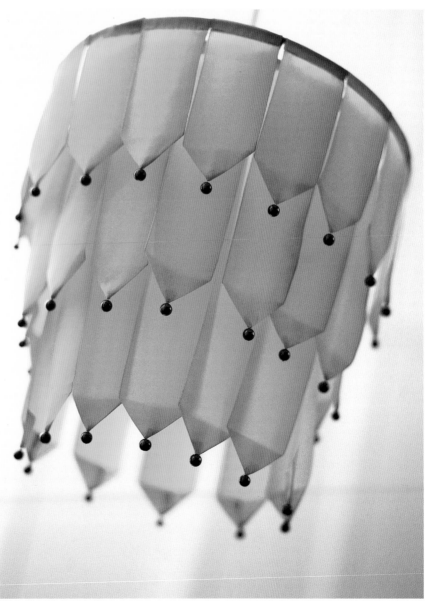

121

linen loose cover

An ornate wall sconce is topped with a piece of the palest apricot linen no bigger than a pocket handkerchief. The soft-hued, fluid fabric sits loosely on a card shade and looks as if it has just floated down and settled in place, creating a gentle pool of background light for a relaxed and intimate atmosphere.

materials & equipment

card undershade with bulb fitting: 3 in. (8 cm) diameter top; 7 in. (18 cm) diameter bottom; 5 in. (13 cm) height

20 in. (50 cm) apricot linen, 45 in. (115 cm) wide

pattern paper

compass, or pencil, drawing pin, and string

gingham in gathers

For a lampshade like this miniature square, a small-scale pattern such as gingham is ideal. To give the tiny shade a little more impact, the fabric has been very tightly gathered all around the top and bottom, and matching braid has been attached to finish the edges and add a decorative touch.

materials & equipment

square frame with four side struts and clip fixture: 3 ½ in. (9 cm) square top; 5 in. (13 cm) square bottom; 4 in. (10 cm) height

20 in. (50 cm) blue and white gingham, 45 in. (115 cm) wide

20 in. (50 cm) white silk lampshade lining, 45 in. (115 cm) wide

½ in. (1 cm) wide binding tape

1 ¼ yd. (100 cm) decorative braid

fabric adhesive

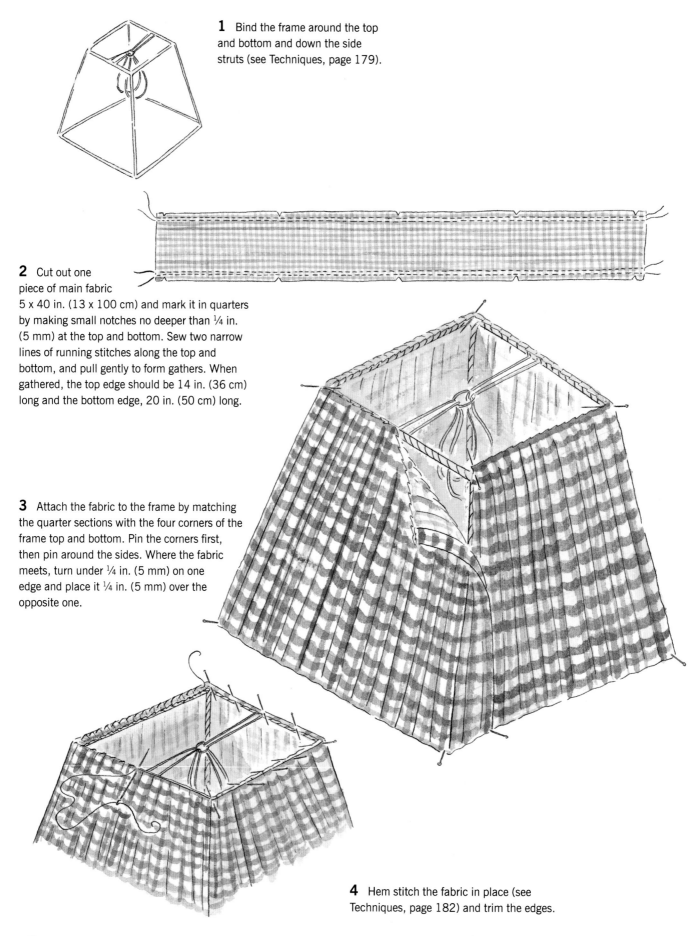

1 Bind the frame around the top and bottom and down the side struts (see Techniques, page 179).

2 Cut out one piece of main fabric 5 x 40 in. (13 x 100 cm) and mark it in quarters by making small notches no deeper than ¼ in. (5 mm) at the top and bottom. Sew two narrow lines of running stitches along the top and bottom, and pull gently to form gathers. When gathered, the top edge should be 14 in. (36 cm) long and the bottom edge, 20 in. (50 cm) long.

3 Attach the fabric to the frame by matching the quarter sections with the four corners of the frame top and bottom. Pin the corners first, then pin around the sides. Where the fabric meets, turn under ¼ in. (5 mm) on one edge and place it ¼ in. (5 mm) over the opposite one.

4 Hem stitch the fabric in place (see Techniques, page 182) and trim the edges.

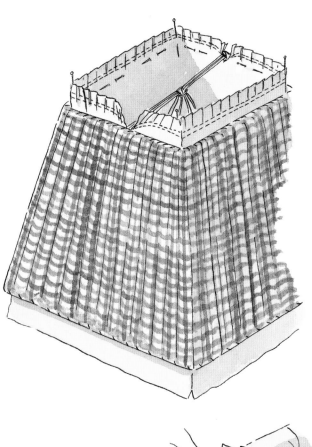

5 To line the shade, cut one piece of silk lining measuring 5½ x 21 in. (14 x 52 cm). Mark into four sections top and bottom, adding a ½-in. (5 mm) seam allowance at the ends. Sew two narrow lines of running stitches along the top to form gathers as in step 2. Then pin the lining to the inside of the shade top and bottom, lining up the sections with the four struts. Pull the raw edges over the frame, making small slits in the top to fit around the arms of the bulb clip.

6 Fold the raw edges under ¼ in. (5 mm), pin and hem stitch in place. Finish the side seams the same way as for the gingham cover.

7 Cut the decorative braid to fit the top and bottom, adding an extra ½-in. (5 mm) overlap. Glue it in place with fabric adhesive, turning under one of the raw ends for neat finish.

striped wall shield

This minute half shade is designed to shield a bulb on a wall sconce. The unusual shape is ideal for elaborate and ornate sconces. The striped silk taffeta is stretched very tightly around the frame, and the same stripe is cut on the bias to trim the edges. The whole project is made with hand stitching only.

materials & equipment

half cylinder frame with bulb clip: 6 ½ in. (16 cm) wide; 5 in. (13 cm) height at center; 4 ½ in. (11 cm) height at sides

30 in. (75 cm) striped silk taffeta, 45 in. (115 cm) wide

10 in. (25 cm) lining fabric, 45 in. (115 cm) wide

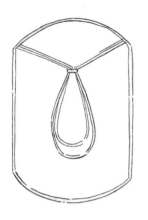

1 Start by binding all around the frame with binding tape (see Techniques, page 179).

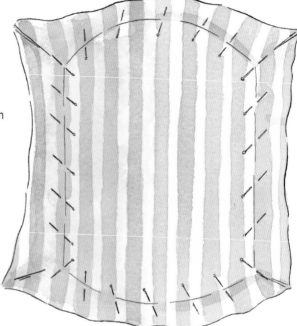

2 Cut a piece of silk taffeta 7 x 8 in. (18 x 20 cm) with the stripes running vertically. Pin the piece around the edge of the front of the frame, pinning first in the center at the top and bottom and on the sides, then at the corners and then at opposite sides around the frame, pulling the fabric tight.

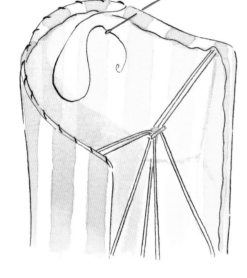

3 Hem stitch (see Techniques, page 182) to the binding all around the frame and trim.

4 Next cut out a 7 x 8 in. (18 x 20 cm) piece of lining. Pin it around the edge of the reverse side of the frame in the same way as for the silk taffeta, overlapping the raw edge of the silk taffeta. Cut slits to fit the fabric around the arms for the bulb clip.

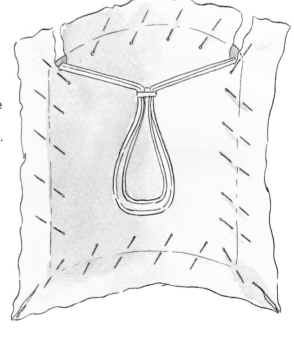

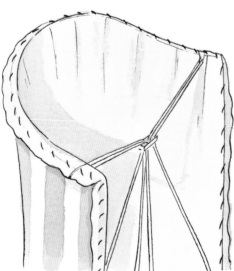

5 Once the pins are in position and the lining is really tight, hem stitch the lining to the binding all around the inside of the frame. Trim away the excess fabric.

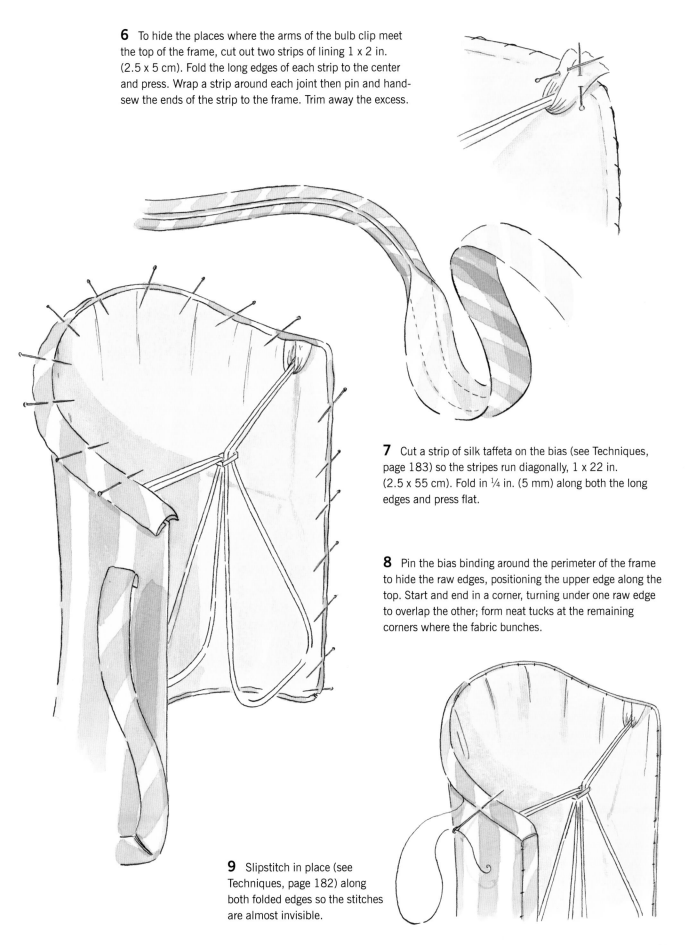

6 To hide the places where the arms of the bulb clip meet the top of the frame, cut out two strips of lining 1 x 2 in. (2.5 x 5 cm). Fold the long edges of each strip to the center and press. Wrap a strip around each joint then pin and hand-sew the ends of the strip to the frame. Trim away the excess.

7 Cut a strip of silk taffeta on the bias (see Techniques, page 183) so the stripes run diagonally, 1 x 22 in. (2.5 x 55 cm). Fold in ¼ in. (5 mm) along both the long edges and press flat.

8 Pin the bias binding around the perimeter of the frame to hide the raw edges, positioning the upper edge along the top. Start and end in a corner, turning under one raw edge to overlap the other; form neat tucks at the remaining corners where the fabric bunches.

9 Slipstitch in place (see Techniques, page 182) along both folded edges so the stitches are almost invisible.

curtains and drapes

use of fabrics

Fabric comes in a wide and dazzling array of colors, textures, and patterns. By piecing together fabric in unexpected combinations, you will achieve innovative and original effects. Be bold, and experiment with different textures and different designs, all cunningly combined in a single pair of curtains. Creative use of fabrics will allow you to make elegant, stylish, and totally unique window treatments.

below *An inexpensive slubby cotton has been lined and interlined for a luxurious and opulent effect. The bobbled border at the top of the curtains creates textural interest.*
below left *Black and white antique toile de Jouy curtains are teamed with an irreverent red bobble fringing to create a timeless look at an elegant window. Unexpected combinations like this will enliven a simple pair of curtains.*

left *A stylish alternative to the ubiquitous white nets. A checked red and white voile serves the same purpose—privacy—but with a little more verve and color.*

below left to right *Ready-made tab-topped curtains are dyed in oranges, yellows, and reds. The fabric filters light and creates a dappled effect. Two pairs of curtains on separate poles, one made from flimsy voile and the other cotton moiré, create an interesting layered look. The narrow edging on these pretty toile de Jouy curtains brings definition to the leading edge and frames an unusual round window; an upholstered slipper chair has been covered in the same fabric and continues the feminine yet unfussy theme. Crisp white cotton allows light to filter into a room, yet provides both privacy and shade.*

yellow checks

These cheerful curtains are guaranteed to bring a sunny atmosphere to any room. They use panels of three coordinating fabrics joined horizontally. A vivid scarlet braid is sewn over the seams to conceal any unsightly joins on the front of the curtain. The bold checks and braid have a pleasing rustic simplicity that is echoed by the ties that hold the curtains to an iron pole.

materials & equipment

three different main fabrics

lining fabric

⅝ in. (1.5 cm) wide red braid

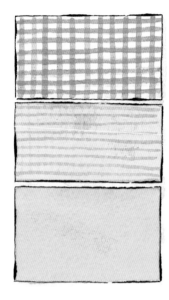

1 Measure the window to calculate fabric quantities (see Techniques, page 180). Each panel occupies one third of the drop of the finished curtain. Add ⅝ in. (1.5 cm) to the length of each panel for each seam. Add another 3 in. (8 cm) to the top panel for the heading and 6½ in. (16 cm) to the bottom panel for the hem. Each curtain must be the width of the pole plus a 4¾-in. (12 cm) hem allowance. The lining fabric must be 1¾ in. (4 cm) smaller than the finished curtain all around. Cut out the fabric.

2 Place the top panel on a flat surface with the middle panel on top, right sides together and raw edges aligned. Pin, baste, and machine stitch the two panels together, using a ⅝ in. (1.5 cm) seam allowance and matching the checks as best you can. Press open the seam. Attach the bottom panel to the middle panel in the same way.

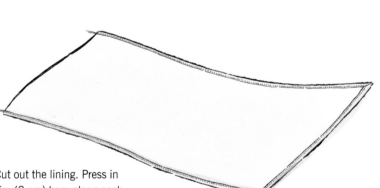

3 Cut two strips of braid to the width of the curtain. Center the braid over the seams between the panels on the right side of the curtain. Pin, baste, and machine stitch down both edges of the braid.

4 Press in a 2½-in. (6 cm) hem at each side of the curtain and a double 3-in. (8 cm) hem at the bottom. Press in the angled miters (see Techniques, page 183). Pin and baste the hems in place. Herringbone stitch the side hems. Slipstitch the bottom hem and the miters.

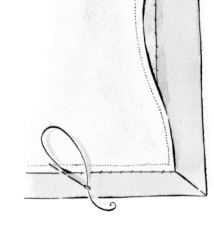

5 Cut out the lining. Press in a ¾-in. (2 cm) hem along each side edge and a double ¾-in. (2 cm) hem along the bottom. Pin and baste the hems. Miter the corners (see Techniques, page 183) and machine stitch the hems in place.

6 Place the curtain on a flat surface, wrong side up. Place the lining on top, right side up. Match the corners of the lining with the mitered corners of the curtain and align the top raw edges. Pin the curtain and lining together along the top raw edges. Pin and baste the lining to the curtain. Slip stitch the lining to the curtain fabric. Leave the bottom of the lining open to make the curtain hang better.

7 The number of ties you will need will depend on the width of the curtain. There should be one tie every 10 in. (25 cm). Cut a strip of fabric, 2½ x 20 in. (6 x 50 cm), for each tie. Make the ties (see Techniques, page 184), and then knot the ends of each one tightly.

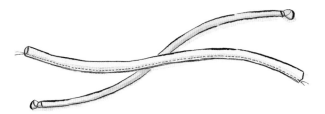

8 Lay the curtain flat, right side up. Using fabric pen, lightly mark a line 3 in. (8 cm) below the top raw edge. Position a tie at each top corner of the curtain and space the other ties at 10-in. (25 cm) intervals in between. Pin and baste the halfway point of each tie to the marked line, then machine stitch all the way along the line, taking in the ties as you go.

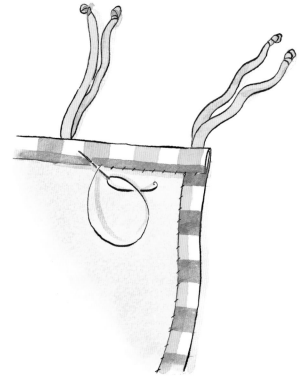

9 Press in a double 1½-in. (4 cm) fold to the wrong side along the top edges of the curtain. Pin, baste, and slipstitch the folded edge of the curtain to the lining.

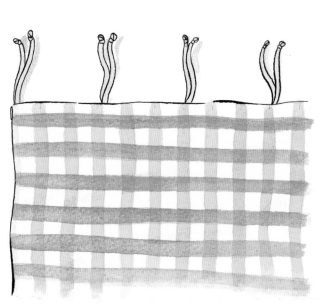

10 Working at the two top corners of the curtain, slipstitch the open ends of the top hem together. Press the finished curtains; then tie them to the pole loosely, adjusting the length to find the right height.

large-hemmed linen drapes

These classic pencil-pleat drapes have an unexpected feature—
a deep hem, in the same fabric but in a contrasting color, which
just rests upon the ground. Adding contrasting hems is a simple
yet effective device, for they bring color and contrast to the
plainest of curtains and add interest to a neutral,
understated color scheme.

materials & equipment

main fabric

contrasting fabric for hem

lining fabric

3-in. (8 cm) wide pencil-pleat heading tape

curtain hooks

1 To figure out how much fabric you will need, measure your window (see Techniques, page 180). These drapes have a pencil-pleat heading, which requires material two and a half to three times the width of the finished curtain. Add 4¾ in. (12 cm) to the width for the side hems. The length of the main material is five-sixths of the drop from pole to floor. Add 3 in. (8 cm) for the heading, and a ⅝-in. (1.5 cm) seam allowance to attach the contrasting hem.

2 The contrasting material for the hem must be the same width as the main panel, plus an additional 4¾ in. (12 cm) for the side hems. The length should be one-sixth of the drop from pole to floor. Add 6½ in. (16 cm) for the hem, and a ⅝-in. (1.5 cm) seam allowance at the top to attach the hem to the main material.

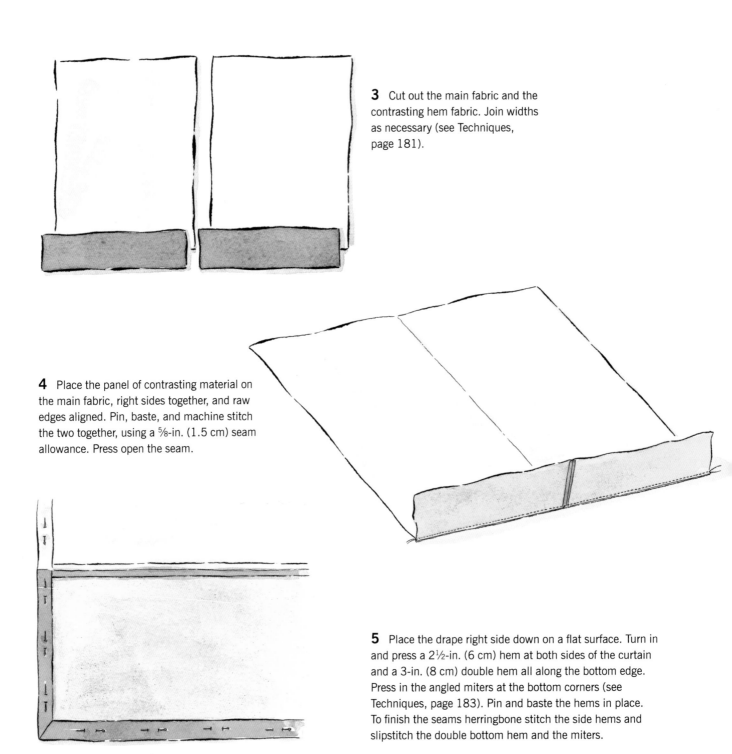

3 Cut out the main fabric and the contrasting hem fabric. Join widths as necessary (see Techniques, page 181).

4 Place the panel of contrasting material on the main fabric, right sides together, and raw edges aligned. Pin, baste, and machine stitch the two together, using a ⅝-in. (1.5 cm) seam allowance. Press open the seam.

5 Place the drape right side down on a flat surface. Turn in and press a 2½-in. (6 cm) hem at both sides of the curtain and a 3-in. (8 cm) double hem all along the bottom edge. Press in the angled miters at the bottom corners (see Techniques, page 183). Pin and baste the hems in place. To finish the seams herringbone stitch the side hems and slipstitch the double bottom hem and the miters.

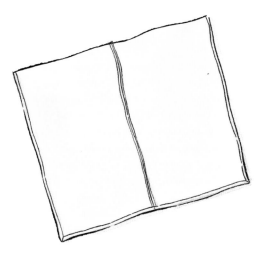

6 The lining should be 1¾ in. (4 cm) smaller all around than the finished drape. Cut out the lining fabric and join widths if necessary (see Techniques, page 183). To finish the edges turn, and press a ¾-in. (2 cm) hem along each side edge of the lining and a double ¾-in. (2 cm) hem along the bottom edge. Miter the corners and press. Pin, baste, and machine stitch the side and bottom hems in place.

7 Place the drape on a flat surface, wrong side up. Place the lining on top of the drape, right side up. Match the corners of the lining to the mitered corners of the main fabric and align the top raw edges. There should be a border of drape fabric showing all around the lining. Pin the drape and lining together along their top raw edges. Pin, baste, and slipstitch the folded edges of the lining to the drape. Leave the bottom of the lining open to make the drape hang better.

8 Cut the pencil-pleat heading tape to the width of the drape plus an additional 1¼ in. (3 cm) at each end. Knot the strings at the leading edge and leave them loose at the other.

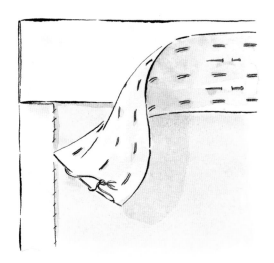

9 At the top raw edge of the drape, turn down a 3-in. (8 cm) fold to the wrong side. Press in place. Position the heading tape along the top of the drape, ½ in. (1 cm) below the folded top edge. Tuck under the raw ends of the tape and the knotted strings at the leading edge. The turnover will be concealed by the heading tape. Pin, baste, and machine stitch around the edges of the heading tape through all the layers of fabric.

10 Pull the strings in the heading tape so that even gathers form across the front of the drape. Knot the ends. Insert the drape hooks into the tape at regular intervals; then hang the drapes from curtain rings or track.

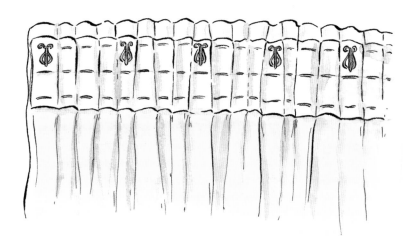

headings

A curtain is attached to a track, rod, or pole by the heading—the decorative top of the curtain. From formal pleated headings hung from antique poles with elaborate gilt finials to informal ties loosely knotted around an iron rod, a heading sets the mood for the curtains. A wide variety of heading tapes is now available, so creating pinch pleats, goblet pleats, soft gathers, and many other heading styles is now easier and more achievable than ever before.

A variety of headings:
far left *Red-checked voile with a cased heading for a softly gathered effect.*
left *Pinch pleats create an elegant, formal feel.*
below left *Gathering tape gives a gently ruffled heading.*

below far left *A tightly gathered pencil pleat heading gives a ruched effect that adds interest to plain cream curtains.*
below center *A simple heading with rings attached to hooks.*
below right *Unusual double curtains are attached to a pair of poles by means of clip-on curtain rings, which require no sewing.*
bottom *A crisp check curtain with neatly knotted ties.*

above and above left *Two examples of knotted ties. This is a simple and informal style of heading that works very well when curtains are not too weighty. Curtains with a tie heading must be drawn manually.*

left *A sunshine yellow ticking with a tiny loop heading is strung across the bottom half of a window on string knotted to brass-headed nails.*

below left *Slotted onto a length of vivid braided red string, this checked curtain with a cased heading has a casual utilitarian feel.*

below *A simple cream curtain hanging from a classic wooden pole is enlivened by the addition of a chenille bobble fringe all along the loosely gathered heading.*

reversible scallops

These cozy quilted curtains could not be simpler to make.
The fabric is reversible, so the curtains do not require a lining,
and the scalloped top of the curtain simply flops over to act as a
valance, showing the other side of the fabric. The curtains are
attached to the pole with unobtrusive brass curtain clips,
dispensing with the need for a sewn heading.

materials & equipment

reversible quilted fabric

bias binding

brass curtain clips

tie-on sheers

These floaty curtains hanging at a French door create a light and airy effect. The wrought-iron pole is attached to the ceiling, and the length of the curtains and the swathes of fabric emphasize rather than obscure the fine proportions of the elegant glass doors. The bobbly tassel fringe provides a textural contrast with the economical outlines of the simple metal tieback.

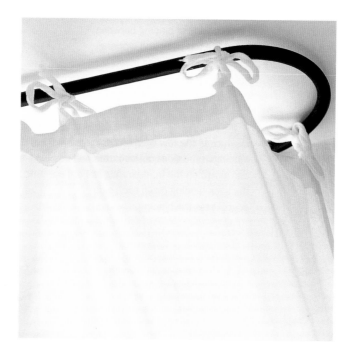

materials & equipment

white voile

tassel fringe

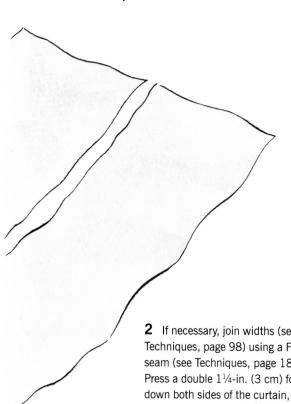

1 To calculate the amount of fabric required, measure the window (see Techniques, page 180). The width of each single curtain must be equal to the entire length of the pole to give enough fullness in the width. Add 4¾ in. (12 cm) to the width for side hems and 9 in. (22 cm) to the length for hem and heading. Cut out the fabric (see Techniques, page 180).

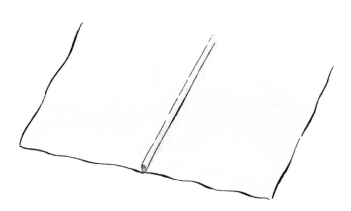

2 If necessary, join widths (see Techniques, page 98) using a French seam (see Techniques, page 183). Press a double 1¼-in. (3 cm) fold down both sides of the curtain, and pin, baste, and machine stitch in place.

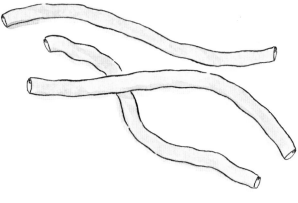

3 The number of ties needed will depend on the width of the curtain, but there should be one tie approximately every 6 in. (15 cm). Cut out strips of voile, each one 2 x 18 in. (5 x 45 cm), and make the ties for each curtain (see Techniques, page 184).

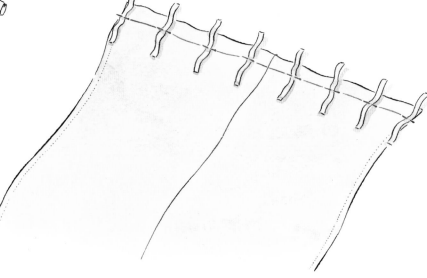

4 Place the curtain right side up on a flat surface, and mark a line across the curtain, 4¾ in. (12 cm) below the top raw edge. Position a tie at each top corner of the curtain and space the other ties evenly between them. Pin and baste the midpoint of each tie to the line, then machine stitch all the way along the marked line, securing the ties to the curtain.

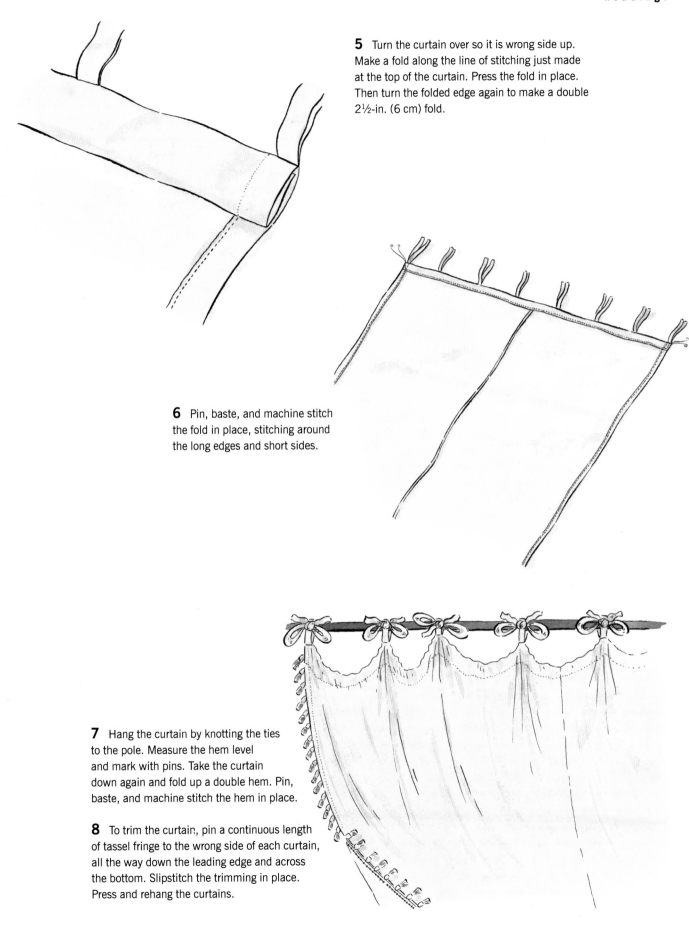

5 Turn the curtain over so it is wrong side up. Make a fold along the line of stitching just made at the top of the curtain. Press the fold in place. Then turn the folded edge again to make a double 2½-in. (6 cm) fold.

6 Pin, baste, and machine stitch the fold in place, stitching around the long edges and short sides.

7 Hang the curtain by knotting the ties to the pole. Measure the hem level and mark with pins. Take the curtain down again and fold up a double hem. Pin, baste, and machine stitch the hem in place.

8 To trim the curtain, pin a continuous length of tassel fringe to the wrong side of each curtain, all the way down the leading edge and across the bottom. Slipstitch the trimming in place. Press and rehang the curtains.

valances

Valances add a perfect finishing touch to an attractive window treatment and can be major decorative elements in their own right. Valances can be stiffened and shaped pieces of fabric hung from a board, or softer in effect and unstiffened. They can be used alone or teamed with matching or contrasting drapes.

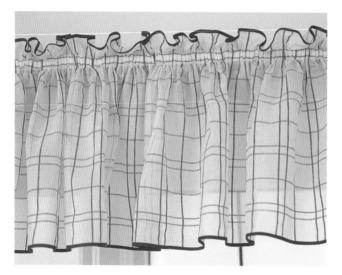

left *A checked voile valance is edged top and bottom with a thin red trim, which emphasizes the tight ruffles of the gathering tape heading. Valances are ideally suited to windows that do not need a full curtain.*

below left *This panel of fabric acts as a valance at a small kitchen window. Small-scale red-and-white gingham has a cased heading into which an expansion rod has been inserted. The fabric is held out of the way with thin ties. A quick and easy window treatment that need not be a permanent fixture.*

below *An unassuming pair of striped cotton curtains is made much more immposing by the addition of a classic shaped valance. Vertically striped curtains and valances can appear to lengthen the proportions of small, wide windows.*

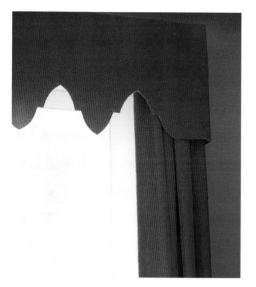

above *A bold Gothic-inspired valance covered in a rich red linen. This type of valance uses buckram, a stiffened hessian fabric that can hold the desired shape. Shaped and stiffened valances such as this one are guaranteed to add an air of importance to a window treatment and are especially useful for screening an unsightly window top.*

above center *This cheerful checked curtain is self-valanced—the valance is a separate piece of the same fabric sewn to the top of the curtain. Heading tape has been attached to the back of the curtain just below the seam. A contrasting border defines the leading edge of the curtains and the bottom of the valance.*

above right *A more traditional and formal valance treatment. A wooden valance board has been covered tightly with fabric that matches the curtains, then attached to the wall just above the curtain track with a pair of brackets. The box-pleated skirt has been either stapled or velcro'd to the valance board. The valance is trimmed with narrow binding in a complementary color.*

right *In a small bathroom, the window is screened by a sheer fabric panel and deep valance, which do not block the light as conventional curtains do. The bold valance, with its scalloped edges, is made from large-scale gingham checks and edged with small-scale gingham cut on the bias.*

monogrammed linen valance

This linen valance has been decorated with a machine-embroidered initial, but its fluid folds and majestic proportions would be just as effective if it were plain. The valance is designed to hang alone, but can be combined with unlined curtains in the same fabric, suspended from eyelets screwed into the bottom of the valance board.

materials & equipment

heavy linen fabric

lining fabric

staple gun

¾-in. (2 cm) thick plywood for the mounting board

angled shelf brackets

rope-edged valance

The jolly stripes, wavy bottom, and coordinating rope trim of this slightly gathered valance give it a cheerful nautical air. It is an ideal summer replacement for heavy full-length curtains. The valance allows plenty of summer sunlight to flood into the room, yet prevents the window from looking too bare and unfurnished.

materials & equipment

striped cotton fabric

thick rope trim

1 To calculate fabric quantities, measure the window (see Techniques, page 180). The length of the pole will dictate the finished width of the valance. The valance should hang down over about a fifth of the window. Add an extra ⅝-in. (1.5 cm) seam allowance all around. Cut out two pieces of fabric, one for the front and one for the back of the valance. Remember that the stripes should run vertically.

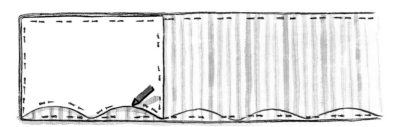

2 Make a template for the bottom edge of the valance (see Templates, page 181). Pin the front and back panels of fabric right sides together, then pin the template to the back panel. Draw around the template.

3 With the two panels still pinned together, cut along the marked line through both layers of fabric.

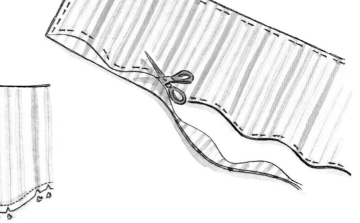

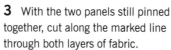

4 Baste and machine stitch along the sides and curved bottom edge of the panel, using a ⅝-in. (1.5 cm) seam allowance. Leave the top straight edge open. Trim the seam allowance and clip the curves and corners of the curved edge to reduce any puckering or bulkiness.

5 The number of ties you need will depend on the width of your valance, but you should have a tie above every "wave" along the bottom of the valance and one at each corner. Make the ties (see Techniques, page 184) and knot the ends of each tie.

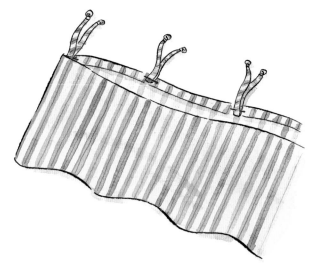

6 Turn the valance right side out. All around the top edges of the valance press a ⅝-in. (1.5 cm) fold to the inside. Fold each tie in half widthwise and tuck them between the top folded edges, positioning a tie at each end of the valance and spacing them at regular intervals in between.

7 Pin and baste the ties to the inside of the folded edges. Machine stitch the two top edges of the valance together, close to the folded edge and taking in all the ties.

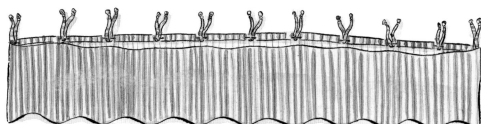

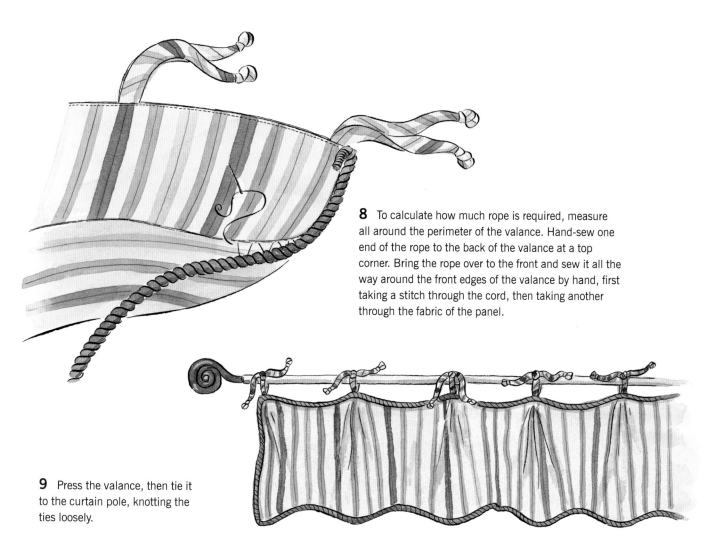

8 To calculate how much rope is required, measure all around the perimeter of the valance. Hand-sew one end of the rope to the back of the valance at a top corner. Bring the rope over to the front and sew it all the way around the front edges of the valance by hand, first taking a stitch through the cord, then taking another through the fabric of the panel.

9 Press the valance, then tie it to the curtain pole, knotting the ties loosely.

edgings

Adding an edging or border to a curtain will create an additional decorative element and subtly enliven even the most understated window treatment. From subtle scallops to tasseled trim, edgings should be chosen to complement yet contrast with your curtain. And always remember that bold and simple edgings are more effective than fuss and flounce.

below left top and bottom *Shaggy silk fringe attached to the leading edge brings an intriguing tactile quality to a plain pair of curtains.*
below center *A translucent voile panel edged with a wide grosgrain ribbon screens the view, yet does not obscure the elegant lines of this window and full-length shutters.*
below *The backs of curtains are rarely as attractive as the fronts. However, these are decorative on both sides. The front of the curtain is a cheerful blue gingham while the back has a bold border.*

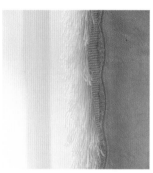

left, right, and above *When used as an edging, bobble fringe adds an interesting textural element to any soft furnishings and will instantly transform even the dullest pair of curtains. It is available in a wide variety of colors and weights, making it a suitable trimming for almost every fabric. Attached to the leading edge of a curtain, it will add definition and interest.*

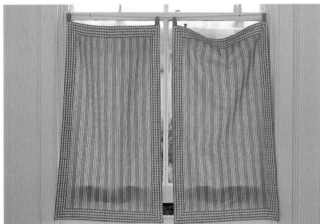

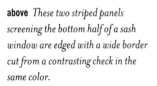

above *These two striped panels screening the bottom half of a sash window are edged with a wide border cut from a contrasting check in the same color.*

right *A simple pair of floaty voile curtains are given an opulent, elegant feel with the addition of a fluffy tasseled fringe.*

far right *A printed border sewn to the bottom of plain cotton curtains imitates the effect of handstitched embroidery.*

167

squares on squares

Ideally suited to a small or recessed window, the cheerful checked borders make the curtains into a focal point without swamping the window in folds of fabric. Unobtrusive ties in the same checked fabric as the border hold the curtains to a narrow metal pole, with heart-shaped finials that contribute to the overall air of harmonious simplicity.

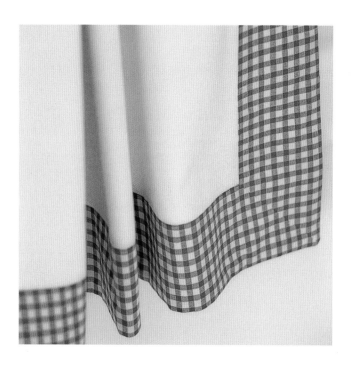

materials & equipment

heavy cotton fabric

checked cotton for the border and ties

1 To calculate how much fabric you will need, measure the window (see Techniques, page 180). A single width of fabric may be enough for each curtain if you have a small window, but you will have to join widths if your windows are larger (see Techniques, page 181). The curtains are self-lined, so the back panel is made from the same fabric as the front panel.

2 The front panel of main fabric for each curtain should be 6 in. (15 cm) smaller all around than the back panel, to allow for the border. Cut out the fabric for the front and back panels.

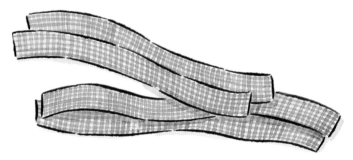

3 For the border cut four strips of fabric, two 8 in. (20 cm) deep and the same length as the back panel, and the other two 8 in. (20 cm) deep and the same width as the back panel.

4 Place one strip on top of another with right sides together. Pin and baste the strips together at a 45° angle from the top corner, stopping ⅝ in. (1.5 cm) from the bottom edge. Check that the angle of the seam is correct, then machine stitch together. Trim the seams.

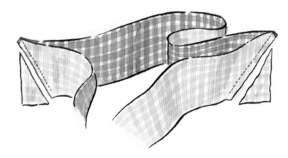

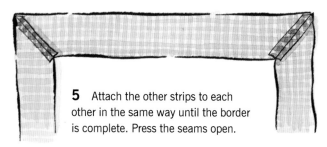

5 Attach the other strips to each other in the same way until the border is complete. Press the seams open.

6 Place the back panel on a flat surface, right side up. Place the border on top, right side down. Pin the two together all around the perimeter.

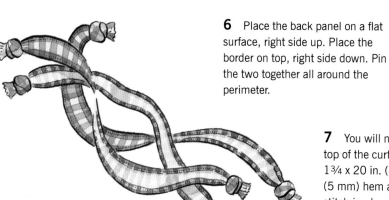

7 You will need one tie every 6 in. along the top of the curtain. Cut strips of checked fabric, 1¾ x 20 in. (4 x 50 cm). Press in a ¼-in. (5 mm) hem all around the edges and machine stitch in place. Knot the ends of each tie.

8 Fold the ties in half widthwise and press. Unpin the top of the border and insert the ties between the back panel and the border, placing one tie at each corner and spacing them at regular 6-in. (15 cm) intervals in between. Line up the fold of the tie with the raw edge of the curtain, the knotted ends of the ties pointing in toward the center of the curtain.

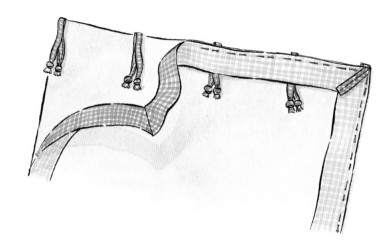

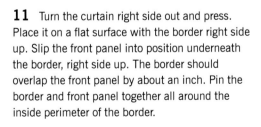

9 When all the ties are in place, baste and machine stitch the back panel and the border together around all four sides, using a ⅝-in. (1.5 cm) seam allowance. Take in all the ties as you stitch.

10 Press a ⅝-in. (1.5 cm) hem to the wrong side all around the inside raw edges of the border, trimming the corners.

11 Turn the curtain right side out and press. Place it on a flat surface with the border right side up. Slip the front panel into position underneath the border, right side up. The border should overlap the front panel by about an inch. Pin the border and front panel together all around the inside perimeter of the border.

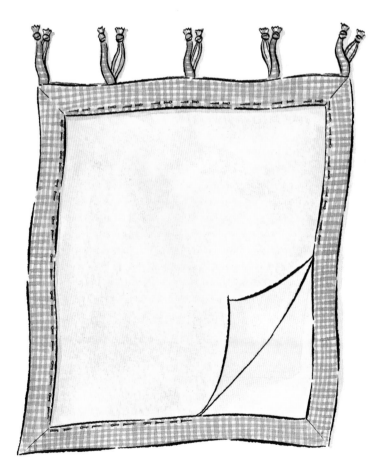

12 Check that the curtain lies flat and smooth before you baste and machine stitch the two layers together from the right side, stitching close to the inside folded edge of the border. Press the curtain and hang it by knotting the ties loosely around a curtain pole.

contrasting scalloped border

An elegant scalloped black felt border provides a striking
textural contrast to the crisp clean folds and snowy white cotton
of these floor-length curtains. The border adds definition
to the pale curtains and frames the view from the window.
The curtains are lined and interlined to give them a luxurious
padded thickness.

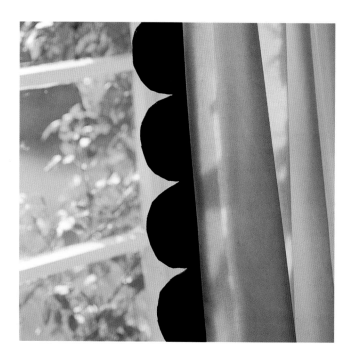

materials & equipment

white herringbone cotton

interlining

lining fabric

thick black felt

2-in. (5 cm) wide pencil-pleat heading tape

curtain hooks

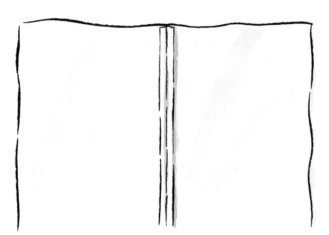

1 To calculate fabric quantities, measure the window (see Techniques, page 180). The curtains have a pencil-pleat heading and require fabric two and a half times the length of the pole. Add 6½ in. (16 cm) to the length for hem and heading, and 4¾ in. (12 cm) to the width for side hems. The interlining must be the same size as the curtain without additions for hems. The lining must be 1¾ in. (4 cm) smaller than the finished curtain all around. Cut out the main fabric, lining, and interlining, and join widths (see Techniques, page 181).

2 Make a template for the scalloped border (see Templates, page 181). Cut two strips of felt, each 4 in. (10 cm) deep and the same length as the finished curtain. Place the template on top and mark around it, then cut along the outline.

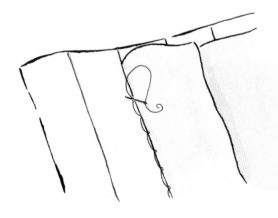

3 Lay the curtain right side up and, using fabric pen, mark a line all the way down one side of the curtain, 2½ in. (6 cm) in from the raw edge. Place the straight edge of the felt strip along this line, the scallops sitting on the inside, the top of the strip 3 in. (8 cm) below the top of the curtain and the end of the strip 3 in. (8 cm) above the bottom of the curtain.

4 Pin, baste, and machine stitch the felt to the curtain, ½ in. (1 cm) from the straight edge, then zigzag stitch the straight edge of the felt so it lies flat and is unobtrusive.

5 Place the curtain right side down. Use a ruler and fabric pen to mark a series of vertical lines, each 12 in. (30 cm) apart, across the back of the curtain.

6 Place the interlining on the curtain, 3 in. (8 cm) below the top edge and 3 in. (8 cm) above the bottom edge. Fold back the interlining until the fold aligns with the first line; then lock-stitch the interlining to the curtain. Continue until the interlining is locked in all the way across the main fabric.

7 Press in a 2½-in. (6 cm) hem over the interlining at each side edge of the curtain and a 3-in. (8 cm) along the bottom edge. Press the angled miters (see Techniques, page 100) at the bottom corners of the curtain. The scallops should now sit along the outer edge of the curtain.

8 Pin and baste the hems. Loosely herringbone stitch the side and bottom hems and slipstitch the miters in place.

9 Cut out the lining and join widths if necessary (see Techniques, page 98). Turn and press a ¾-in. (2 cm) fold along the side edges of the lining and a double ¾-in. (2 cm) hem along the bottom. Miter the corners and press. Pin, baste, and machine stitch the side and bottom hems in place.

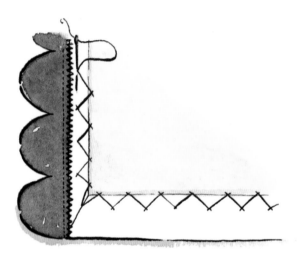

10 Place the curtain on a flat surface, interlined side up. Put the lining on top, right side up. Match the corners of the lining with the mitered corners of the main fabric and align the top edges. There should be a border of fabric showing all around the lining. Pin the lining and curtain together along the top edges. Baste the lining to the curtain, then slipstitch along the folded side edges. Leave the bottom of the lining open to help the curtain hang better.

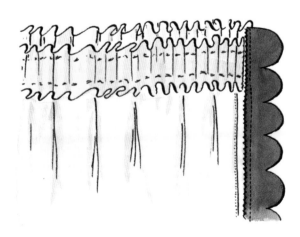

11 Cut the heading tape to the width of the curtain plus 1¼ in. (3 cm) at each end. Knot the strings at the leading edge and leave them loose at the other. At the top of the curtain, turn a 3-in. (8 cm) fold to the wrong side. Pin the tape over the fold, 1¾ in. (4 cm) below the edge, tucking under the raw ends. Pin, baste, and machine stitch the tape in place. Pull the strings and knot the end. Insert the curtain hooks evenly along the length of the tape and hang the curtains.

equipment and techniques

basic techniques

Sewing Kit

For the projects in this book you will need some basic sewing tools. A pair of good-quality fabric shears is essential, as are medium-sized dressmaker's scissors and small embroidery scissors for snipping threads. Pinking shears are useful for finishing raw edges. A metal tape measure, yardstick, and a small plastic ruler, will enable you to measure up accurately.

Invest in good-quality steel dressmaking pins, which will not rust or blunt, and keep them in a box so they stay sharp. A variety of needles, for different weights of fabric, is also essential. Choose your needle according to the weight of the fabric and and the thickness of the thread, and keep a special needle just for embroidery. A steam iron is invaluable during the assembly process, but protect delicate fabrics with a damp cloth. Other useful items to have on hand are a quick-unpick to unpick seams, a blunt knitting needle for pushing out corners, and a thimble.

The projects in this book involve both hand and machine stitches. Basic proficiency in using a sewing machine is necessary, for although it is possible to make many items by hand, it would be a long and laborious process. Your sewing machine should have a good selection of basic stitches. Sophisticated accessories are not needed, but a zipper foot is required for some of the projects in this book. Finally, the process of making home furnishings will be much easier and more enjoyable if you work in a well-lit and well-ventilated area and have a large worktable.

Fabrics

In each project, the fabrics are specified, as the weight, texture, and pattern is suited to the particular design. If you want to use an alternative material, select fabric of a similar weight. Always try to choose fabric that is preshrunk and fade-resistant.

You can find cleaning instructions printed on the selvages of most fabrics in the form of care symbols. Any lined or interlined items must always be dry cleaned, as lining fabric and main fabric tend to shrink at different rates when washed.

The fire-retardant qualities of upholstery fabrics are governed by legislation in many countries. We suggest that you obtain advice from the manufacturer or the retailer of your chosen fabric to make sure your fabric is in line with these regulations.

bed linen

Measuring for bed linen

Before you embark on any of the projects in this book, you must first accurately measure the bed that the item is intended to furnish. This is essential as it will enable you to calculate the size of the finished item and figure out how much fabric you will need to make it. Always take measurements with a metal tape measure (plastic ones can stretch and become inaccurate) and enlist the help of an assistant if the bed is a large one.

Measuring for a pillowcase

Measure the width and length of the pillow. Add 10½ in. (26 cm) flap and seam allowance to the width and 1¼ in. (3 cm) to the length, unless otherwise stated in a project.

Measuring for a bedspread

Measure the bed with bedclothes and pillows in place. For the length, measure from the head to the floor at the foot of the bed. Add an extra 12 in. (30 cm) to tuck behind the pillows. For the width, measure from the floor on one side of the bed over the bed to the floor on the other side. Seam allowances are given in the individual projects.

Measuring for a dust ruffle

Measure the bed base without the mattress. For the length of the central panel (which lies under the mattress), measure the head to the foot of the bed. For the width, measure from one side of the bed base to the other. For the depth of the skirt, measure from the top of the bed base to the floor. The amount of fabric required for the skirt will depend on the desired fullness of the dust ruffle. Seam allowances are given in the individual projects.

Measuring for bedhangings and curtains

If you have a four-poster bed, measure the drop from the bottom of the horizontal supports to the floor for the length of the bedhangings, and the distance between the vertical supports for the width.

If you wish to make a corona or other wall-mounted bed draperies, it is much easier to measure and calculate fabric quantities once the pole or corona board is in place. As a rough guide, they should be positioned approximately 12 in. (30 cm) below the ceiling, but this measurement may have to be adjusted, depending on the proportions of the room. Attach any hardware securely to the wall, using sturdy brackets that will be able to bear the weight of the fixture plus several yards of fabric.

Cutting out the fabric
When making bed linen, or indeed any home furnishings, the fabric must be cut straight, or the finished item will hang crookedly. Unfold the fabric on a flat surface. Use a drafting square and metal ruler to mark a straight line in pencil or fabric pen across the width on the wrong side of the fabric. To cut a width of fabric in half, fold it selvage to selvage and press, then cut along the pressed fold line. If you are using fabric with a high sheen or pile, mark the top of each width with a notch so you can make sure all the fabric will run in the right direction on the finished item.

Joining widths
When making duvets, sheets, or bedspreads, always place a full width panel in the center of the item with equal part or whole widths joined on each side. To join widths, place the widths together, right sides facing, and machine stitch using a ⅝ in. (1.5 cm) seam. Trim the surplus fabric.

Templates for bed projects

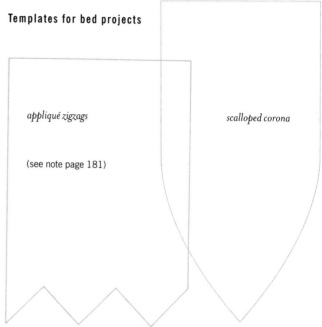

appliqué zigzags

(see note page 181)

scalloped corona

pillows

Pads and fillings
Ready-made pillow forms come in a variety of different shapes and sizes. There are also several different fillings. The most luxurious filling is a combination of feather and down, which should be used sparingly in a puffy scatter cushion or more densely to stuff a firm seat cover. Plastic or latex foam chips tend to be lumpy and uncomfortable, but they are non-absorbent and so are useful for outdoor furnishings. Foam blocks can be cut to size and are used to form squabs for seating; cover the blocks with batting first to smooth out the corners. If you make your own pillow form with a feather filling, use a downproof fabric such as a thick, close-weave cotton, or the sharp feather ends will protrude. Plain cotton or muslin fabric is suitable for pads with a synthetic filling. Do not allow feather or synthetic pads to get wet because they are very absorbent.

Fabrics for pillows and cushions
Choose the type of fabric according to the function of the cushion. Use general upholstery fabrics for most throw pillows, tougher cloth for floor, outdoor, upholstery or squab cushions, and delicate fabrics for more decorative pillows. Try to use preshrunk, colorfast fabric, so you can wash your cover if needed. If you want to use an unusual fabric, check how much it is likely to shrink when washed, since you may need to buy up to a third more material to allow for this process.

Templates for pillow projects

autumnal appliqué

(see note page 181)

lampshades

Frames

There are all manner of shaped frames to choose from. Traditionally, frames were made of wire and then painted or covered with bias binding to prevent rusting, but today most are plastic-coated. When selecting a frame, make sure the style and size are appropriate to the proposed base. You can re-cover an old frame with new fabric if you strip away the old cover, but make sure there are no defects in the basic outline. Shown below are a selection of the most popular frames available with their technical names. You can also buy rings of different diameters, which can be combined with fabrics stiffened by lamination to make cone-shaped frames. This method allows for greater flexibility in shape and size than with ready-made wire cone frames.

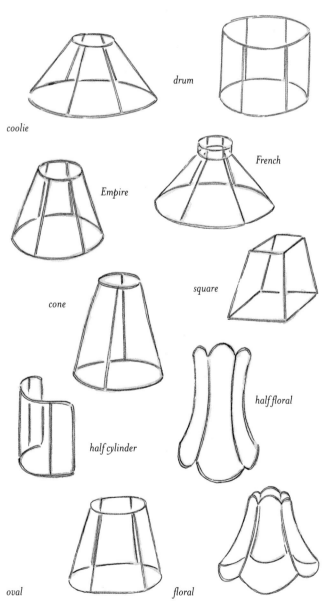

coolie

drum

Empire

French

cone

square

half cylinder

half floral

oval

floral

Measuring and marking tools

Accurate measuring and marking are essential aspects of lampshade making, as it is vital to make sure the cover fits neatly on the frame. Use a metal rule for straight edges and a tape measure for curves and longer lengths. For measuring and drawing small circles, use a compass. For larger circles, make your own compass using a piece of string or tape. Insert a thumbtack pin through one end to mark the midpoint of the circle and attach a pencil to the other end. Adjust the length of string or tape according to the diameter you require and pivot the pencil around the pin to draw the circumference. Thick paper or cardboard is ideal for making templates. For more difficult shapes it is easier to make the template by pinning a lining material or thin muslin directly onto the frame to make sure of a close and accurate fit. Use an ordinary pencil, dressmaker's chalk, or a removable fabric marker for marking the pattern.

Adhesives

Work with an appropriate adhesive; use fabric adhesive for joining fabric to fabric and multipurpose glue for attaching all other types of surfaces, such as laminated fabric to a frame. Clothespins are handy for holding glued edges together while drying.

Laminated covers

Stiff covers are made by laminating a fabric with a self-adhesive backing. Slowly peel away the protective paper from the backing and on a flat surface carefully press the wrong side of the fabric to the sticky surface, removing any trapped air by smoothing with your hands from the middle out. Stiffen the fabric first and then cut out the required pattern. Self-adhesive backing is not suitable for use on an openweave fabric because dust gathers between the threads.

Fabric covers

The type of material you choose will affect the quality of light shed by the shade. White and light solid colors radiate maximum light, while dark colors and patterns obscure light. Stick to smaller repeats since large-scale patterns will be lost on all but the biggest shades. Lightweight cotton and silk are ideal for tight-fitting shades as they have give in them to aid stretching onto the frame. Geometric patterns such as checks should be cut and applied on the bias since it is difficult to achieve really straight vertical and horizontal lines. By positioning the checks at an angle, the eye will not detect a slight lack of symmetry. Try to use an economical width of fabric for the shade, or piece panels together, pattern matching as necessary. Fabric on a shaped frame will fit better if it is first cut into smaller pieces and then joined into panels. Pleated and gathered covers are deceptive; they require a lot more fabric than tight covers, often two or three times as much, so calculate amounts carefully and allow for seam allowances when you are joining pieces together.

Linings

These are generally used in white or cream to allow for maximum reflection of light. The lining helps to hide the struts and the outline of the bulb. Use a strong, non-tear, heat-resistant fabric such as fine Shantung or Japanese silk, satin or crepe. Acetate is a good alternative, although this is more liable to tear. Flame-retardant spray is available for treating the lining. No lining is required on a laminated shade or when you use very heavy fabrics, but with lightweight fabrics like voile or lace, lining is essential to help diffuse light and give substance to the cover.

Trimmings

Many lampshades are finished with a trimming, to hide unsightly stitching, finish raw edges, and provide decoration. Bobble fringe, braid, ribbon, rope, tassels, and piping are just some options, and they can be glued or handsewn in place. Measure the section to be trimmed with a tape measure and add at least 1 in. (2.5 cm) to finish the ends. For removable covers, check the washability and dyes of the trimming. It is a good idea to prewash all fabrics and trimmings before making the cover, to insure even shrinkage and to avoid colors running into each other.

Fixtures

When you have decided on the size and shape of your frame, you must consider the internal fixtures that hold the frame on the support; these are available in various sizes. Your choice of fixture will depend on the function of the shade: for instance, a pendant fixture is necessary for hanging shades, whereas a reversible gimbal is used on table lamps, allowing them to be tilted when directing light on specific areas. Converters and shade carriers are available if you wish to change the height or use of your shade. Finally the size of your bulb can affect the fixture—the bulb must be hidden from view and sit at a safe distance from the lining to avoid scorching or a fire hazard.

Bulbs

Choose a bulb according to the fixture and the size and style of the shade. The bulb should sit below the level of the top of the shade and not hang below the bottom of the shade. The bulb should be at least 1¼ in. (3 cm) away from the inside of the shade. Be very careful that the bulb does not come closer than this distance, or scorching may occur. The bulb must also be set properly in the fixture to avoid burning. For larger lampshades, use up to 60-watt bulbs, but on smaller shades choose 40-watt or below.

Low-voltage bulbs are long lasting and give a bright light and low heat.

TECHNIQUES

Binding the frame

Binding the frame not only gives a better finish if the shade is seen from above or below, but it also provides a necessary anchor for attaching the fabric cover. In most cases, it is best to use a white or neutral-colored binding, although sometimes a different color may suit the design.

First make sure the frame is the correct shape and free from bends, as any defects will show. Use ½ in. (1 cm) wide binding tape. To calculate how much tape is needed, first measure the length of all the sections to be covered with a tape measure and double the final measurement. To bind the frame, spiral the tape all the way around the frame, always maintaining the same angle and just overlapping each previous wrap. Do not overlap by too much or the binding will become very thick and bulky. The finished binding should have a tight, smooth finish so that when you twist it between thumb and index finger it does not slip or move.

To bind a strut, cut a length of binding tape twice the length of the strut. Turn 1 in. (2.5 cm) of the tape over the top ring and with the cut end pointing down, spiral the tape down. Finish at the base of the strut with a knot.

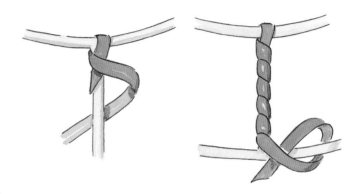

To bind the top and bottom rings of the frame, start by binding a cut end under itself immediately next to a side strut. When you reach a joint with a strut, neatly work the tape around it in a figure-eight pattern. To finish the loose end, fasten with tiny hand stitches and trim away the excess binding.

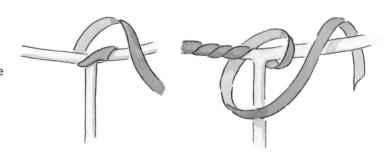

Measuring the frame

To measure any kind of cone-shaped frame, or one that has angled sides, you must first calculate the circumference of the openings at the top and the bottom of the frame by measuring the relevant diameter (the width across each opening) and then multiplying this figure by three. The height of the frame is the angled (not the vertical) height between the top and bottom rings.

curtains

Measuring the window

Before starting to make curtains, you must first measure the window to calculate how much fabric is needed. This is a very important calculation, so take your time and check your measurements again once you have finished.

If possible, mount the track, pole, or valance board in place before measuring the window.

The track or pole should be attached 2–6 in. (5–15 cm) above the window frame, with the ends projecting at least 4 in. (10 cm) beyond each side of the window. Take measurements with a metal tape measure, and if the window is very tall or wide, get someone to help you.

The two measurements needed to calculate fabric quantities for a pair of curtains are the width and the length of the window. To calculate the width of the finished curtains, measure the width of the track, rod, or pole. If you are using a valance board, measure the sides and front. To calculate the drop of finished full-length curtains, measure from the top of the track or bottom of the pole to the floor. For sill-length curtains, measure from the top of the track or bottom of the pole to the sill. For apron-length curtains, measure from the top of the track or pole to just below the sill or to the desired point.

Calculating fabric quantities

Length
The drop from the track, pole, or rod to the floor, sill, or other desired point will determine the length of the finished curtains. Add the appropriate heading and hem allowances (given in the individual projects).
Width
The amount of fabric required is dictated by the curtain heading. Pencil pleat header tape, for example, requires fabric that is two and a half times as wide as the track or pole. Add the allowances for hems and joining widths (given in the individual projects).

To calculate how much fabric you will need for a pair of curtains:

1. Multiply the length of the track or pole by the heading requirement (2½ for pencil pleat heading) to reach the final fabric width.
E.g. Length of the track or pole = 6 ft. (1.8 m)
    Pencil pleat heading = 2½ x length
    Width of fabric = 6 x 2½ = 15 ft. (4.5 m)
2. Divide this measurement by the width of your fabric to calculate how many widths of fabric are required.

Round up the final figure to the next full width.
E.g. Width of chosen fabric = 54 in. (135 cm)
    Width of fabric needed = 15 ft. (4.5 m)
    15 ft. divided by 54 in. = 3.3
    Rounds up to 4

3. Multiply this figure by the unfinished length of the curtain to find out how much fabric is needed.
E.g. Working drop = 10 ft. (3 m)
    10 x 4 = 40 feet (12 m)
Therefore, the total length of fabric required is 13½ yd. (4.2 m), 6¼ yd. (2.1 m) for each curtain.

Allowing for pattern repeats

To match a pattern across a pair of curtains, you need to know the length of the pattern repeat (the fabric supplier will be able to provide you with this information). Divide the unfinished length of each curtain by the length of the repeat, round up the result to the next full figure, then multiply it by the length of the repeat to find out how much fabric you will need.
E.g. The unfinished length of your curtain (including allowances) is 144 in. (355 cm)
    The pattern repeat is 36 in. (90 cm)
    144 divided by 36 = 4
    4 multiplied by 36 = 144
    Each cut length must be 4 yd. (3.7 m) long.

Heading requirements
A few standard heading requirements:

Gathering tape
    2–2.5 times length of track

Pencil pleat tape
    2.5–3 times length of track

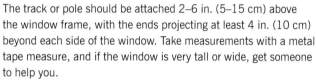

Ties
    1–2 times length of track

Cased heading
    2–3 times length of track

Cutting out the fabric
It is essential that the fabric is cut straight, or the curtain will hang crooked. Place the fabric on a flat surface. Use a metal ruler and a drawing square to mark a straight line in pencil or fabric pen on the wrong side of the fabric. Cut along the line. To cut a width in half, fold it selvage to selvage and cut along the fold. If you are using fabric with a high sheen or pile, mark the top of each width with a notch so all the fabric will run in the right direction on the finished curtain.

Joining widths

Always place any half widths at the outside edge of the curtain, with a full width at the leading edge. To join two widths, place them right sides together, and pin, baste, and machine stitch a straight seam ⅝ in. (1.5 cm) from the raw edges. Trim away any surplus material. If the fabric puckers, it is best to unpick the seam and start again.

Matching patterns across joined widths

On one width of the patterned fabric, fold under a ⅝ in. (1.5 cm) seam allowance to the wrong side and press. Lay the other piece of fabric on a flat surface, right side up. Place the fabric with the folded edge on the second piece of fabric and carefully match the pattern. Pin in place across the fold.

Calculating the size of a valance board

A valance board should be approximately 5–7 in. (13–18 cm) deep, so the curtains project far enough beyond the window. It must be the width of the window frame plus 4 in. (10 cm) to give clearance at each end.

Making a valance board

Using a small saw or jigsaw, cut a piece of plywood or composite board to the required proportions and sand any rough edges. Attach a pair of angle brackets to the underside of the board. This is now the back edge. Two brackets will support a short board; use three or four brackets if you have a long or heavy board. If the board is visible behind the curtains, it must be covered. Cut a piece of matching fabric large enough to cover the board, lay it on a flat surface, wrong side up, and place the board in the center. Fold the fabric over the board as if it were a present and staple it neatly in place, using a heavy-duty staple gun. Use a drill to attach the board firmly to the wall.

Templates for curtan projects

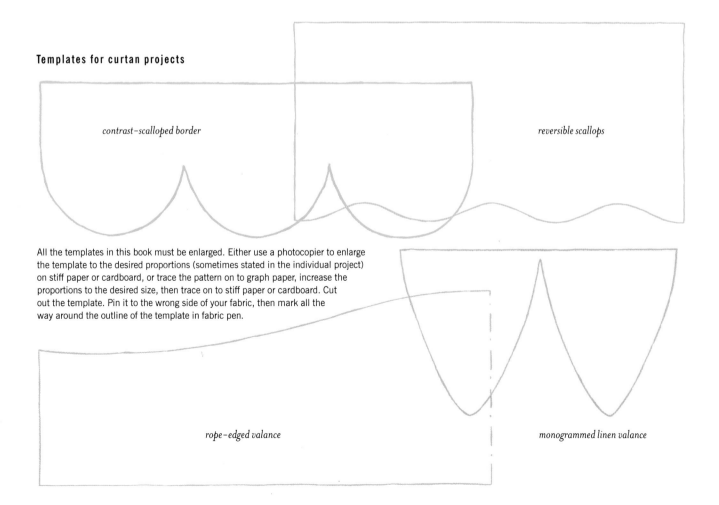

contrast-scalloped border

reversible scallops

rope-edged valance

monogrammed linen valance

All the templates in this book must be enlarged. Either use a photocopier to enlarge the template to the desired proportions (sometimes stated in the individual project) on stiff paper or cardboard, or trace the pattern on to graph paper, increase the proportions to the desired size, then trace on to stiff paper or cardboard. Cut out the template. Pin it to the wrong side of your fabric, then mark all the way around the outline of the template in fabric pen.

basic sewing techniques

STITCHES

Basting stitch

This temporary stitch is like a larger, looser version of running stitch. It holds fabric in place until it is permanently stitched. Use a contrasting thread so the basting is clearly visible and easy to remove.

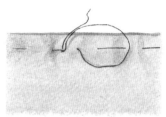

Running or gathering stitch

A series of small, neat stitches, equal in length on both sides of the fabric. Running stitch is used to gather cloth by hand. Knot the thread at one end and sew two parallel rows of running stitches close together along the length to be gathered. Wind the loose threads at the other end around a pin and pull gently to form even gathers.

Slipstitch

Slipstitch holds a folded edge to flat fabric or two folded edges together, as in a mitered corner. Work on the wrong side of the fabric, from right to left. Start with the needle in the

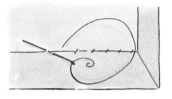

fold. Push it out and pick up a few threads from the flat fabric, then insert it into the hem again, all in one smooth and continuous movement. When finished, the stitches should be almost invisible.

Herringbone stitch

This stitch is used to hold a raw edge to flat fabric. Work from left to right on the wrong side of the fabric, with the needle pointing from right to left. Start with the needle in

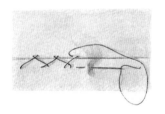

the hem. Push it through the hem and bring the needle diagonally up to the flat fabric. Take a small backward stitch in the flat fabric, about ¼ in. (5 mm) above the hem, picking up just a couple of threads. Bring the needle diagonally back down to the hem, then make a small backward stitch through one thickness of the fabric. Keep the stitches loose.

Hem stitch

Hem stitch should be used to join fabric to the binding tape wrapped around a lampshade frame or to hold a folded edge to a flat fabric. Catch a couple of threads from the flat fabric, then with the needle pointing

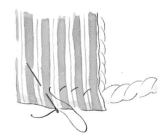

diagonally from right to left, slide it under the fabric and bring it up through the binding tape.

Buttonhole stitch

This stitch is used for buttonholes or wherever a raw edge needs to be finished or strengthened. Work on the right side of the fabric and

stitch with the raw edge of the buttonhole uppermost. Push the needle through the fabric, from back to front, approximately ⅛ in. (3 mm) below the raw edge. Twist the thread around the tip of the needle then pull the needle through to form a knot at the raw edge of the fabric. Always keep the stitches evenly spaced.

Cross stitch

Where possible, work decorative cross stitches in a row, first stitching one half of the cross, then returning back along the row to complete the stitch.

Feather stitch

This decorative stitch should be worked on the right side of the fabric. Bring the needle through at A, insert at B, and bring through again at C, looping the thread underneath the needle before pulling it through. Mirror the process by inserting the needle at D, coming out again at E, and looping the thread underneath the needle again. Repeat this pattern, alternating the looped stitches on each side of the central line.

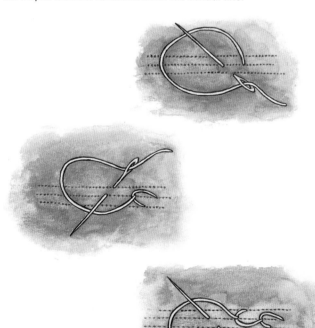

SEAMS

Flat seam

This seam is used to join pieces of fabric. Place the two pieces of fabric right sides together, aligning the edges that are to be seamed. Pin and baste, then machine stitch the seam. Reverse the stitches at the beginning and end of the seam to secure it in place.

Flat-fell seam

This is a sturdy seam for joining heavy fabric. Pin the fabrics right sides together and baste along the seam line. Machine stitch the seam, then press it to one side. Trim the underneath seam to half its width. Fold the upper seam allowance over the trimmed one and baste. Machine stitch in place close to the folded edge.

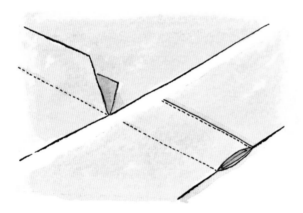

French seam

This self-finishing seam contains all raw edges and is used for sheers and lightweight fabrics. Place two pieces of fabric wrong sides together, aligning the raw edges that are to be seamed. Pin, baste, and machine stitch a seam close to the raw edge. Trim the seam. Fold the material right sides together and then pin, baste and machine stitch a second seam ½ in. (1 cm) from the first, enclosing the raw edges in a narrow tube of fabric.

Double hem

A double hem encloses raw edges and lies flat against the back of fabric. For a 4 in. (10 cm) double hem, the hem allowance will be 8 in. (20 cm). Press the hem allowance along the edge of the fabric. Open out the hem and fold the raw edge up to the pressed line. Fold up again and stitch in place.

Mitering corners

Mitering is the neatest way of working hem corners. Press the hem allowance along the bottom and sides of the fabric then open it out flat again. Where the two fold lines meet, turn in the corner of the fabric diagonally. Turn in the hems along the pressed fold to form a neat diagonal line. Use slipstitch to secure.

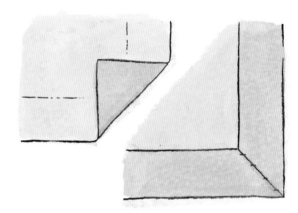

Making an angled miter

An angled miter is necessary when a double bottom hem is wider than the side hems. Press the hem allowance along the bottom and sides of the fabric, then open out again. Fold the corner of the fabric in toward the bottom hem. Then make the first fold in the double hem. Fold in the side hem, then make the second fold in the double hem. The folded edges should meet.

Making ties and tabs

To make a tie, cut a strip of material to the desired width and length. Fold the strip in half along the length, wrong sides together, and press. Pin, baste, and machine stitch all along the long side and one short end, leaving the other short end unstitched. Push the tie right side out with a knitting needle. Turn in a ¼ in. (5 mm) fold to the inside of the tie, press in place, and slipstitch the end closed. Tabs are made in exactly the same way—the only difference is that strip of fabric is wider and they are often buttoned, not tied.

Cutting fabric on the bias

Place your chosen fabric on a flat surface, wrong side up. Take one corner and fold it so the end of the fabric is aligned with the selvage, forming a triangle of fabric. The diagonal fold line is the bias line of the fabric.

Making bias binding

Bias binding is an effective and attractive way to enclose raw edges of fabric. It is easy to make. Find the bias line of the fabric as described above, then mark lines parallel to the bias line across the fabric. Cut out the strips and join them to make a continuous strip of bias binding.

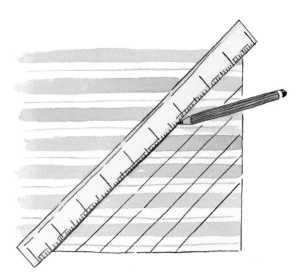

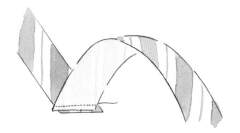

Place two strips, with their right sides together, at right angles, lining up the raw edges. Then machine stitch the two strips together, using a ¼ in. (5 mm) seam allowance. Press flat and cut off the corners.

Making cording

Cording is made from a length of piping cord covered with bias binding. The bias binding must be wide enough to cover the cord and to allow a ⅝ in. (1.5 cm) seam allowance on each side of it. Wrap the binding around the cord, right side out, then machine stitch close to the cord, using a zipper foot.

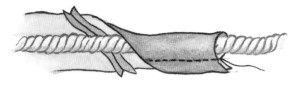

Making box pleats

Box pleats give a tailored finish to curtains, valances, and cushions. One box pleat requires fabric three times the width of the pleat. Decide on the finished width of each pleat, then multiply it by three. The finished width of the object you are making must be divisible by this measurement. For example, if each pleat is 4 in. (10 cm) wide, the width of the item to be pleated must be exactly divisible by 12 in. (30 cm). If it is not, you will have to adjust either the width of the object or the width of the pleat. For a 4 in.(10 cm) pleat, mark a fold 2 in. (5 cm) from the edge of the fabric and another 2 in. (5 cm) from that. Then mark alternate 4 in. (10 cm) and 2 in. (5 cm) folds across the top of the fabric. Fold along the first mark, 2 in. (5 cm) from the edge of the curtain, and bring it across to join a mark 8 in. (20 cm) away from it. Pin the folds together. Leave a 4 in. (10 cm) space and repeat the action all the way across the width of the fabric.

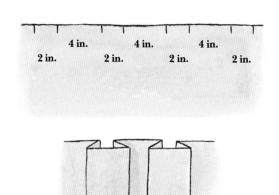

glossary

APPLIQUÉ Applying a second layer of fabric to a main fabric, usually with decorative stitching.

BATTING Thick, soft padding material, made from natural or synthetic fibers, and used for upholstery and quilting.

BIAS BINDING A strip of cloth cut on the bias, at 45° to the selvage, which gives stretch to the fabric. Used as an edging, to bind frames, or to cover piping cord.

BOBBLE FRINGE Tufted ball attached to a length of trimming.

BOLSTER A long cylindrical pillow or cushion with flat ends.

BOX PLEAT A flat, symmetrical pleat formed by folding the fabric to the back at each side of the pleat.

BRAID A woven ribbon used for trimming or edging an item.

BUCKRAM Coarse cloth, stiffened with size and used to give rigidity to valances.

CASING A curtain heading in which a sleeve of material is left open at the top of the curtain to receive a curtain rod or pole.

CHENILLE Tufted and soft velvety yarn; wool, cotton, or synthetic.

CORONA A circular or semicircular structure mounted on the wall above a bed or sofa with draperies suspended from it.

COTTON A natural fiber made from the boll of the cotton plant.

FELT Unwoven cloth made from pounded wool; the edges do not fray after cutting.

FINIAL A decorative fixture attached to each end of a curtain pole.

FLANGE A flat rim or border running around a pillow or cushion.

GATHERS Puckers or folds made by pulling gently on a loosely stitched thread.

GAUFRAGE A pattern branded onto the surface of velvet.

GIMBAL The device attached to the inside of a lampshade frame that holds the shade on the base or the bulb.

GINGHAM A plain-weave two-color cotton cloth with a check pattern.

HEADING The top of a curtain, finished with tape, ties, rings, or other treatments.

HEAD TAPE Ready-made tape that is attached to the top of a curtain to create a particular heading.

INTERLINING Soft material, used as backing or inner lining, gives a luxurious quality.

KNIFE PLEAT A narrow, sharply folded pleat with a straight edge.

LAMINATE A thin protective covering, bonded to a material.

LINEN A strong and flexible fabric spun from the fibers of the flax plant.

LINING FABRIC A secondary fabric used to back curtains, valances, and bedspreads to protect them from light and dust. Usually a cotton or synthetic sateen fabric with a slight sheen.

MADRAS COTTON Striped and checked fine Indian cotton, usually in bright colors.

MATELASSE A thick double cotton cloth, stitched at regular intervals to create a luxurious quilted effect.

MITER The neat diagonal joining of two pieces of fabric where they meet at a corner.

ORGANDY A fine, sheer, fabric made with cotton yarns.

ORGANZA A stiff, transparent fabric.

PENCIL PLEAT HEADING A popular curtain header tape that creates regular, stiff pleats.

PIPING A length of cord covered with bias binding and used as a decorative edging.

PIQUÉ A type of weave that produces a hard-wearing cloth with a ribbed texture and crisp finish.

PLEAT A fold or crease that has been pressed or stitched in place.

PROVENÇAL PRINT French country print on cotton, characterized by small motifs.

RAW EDGE The cut edge of fabric, without selvage or hem.

RUFFLE A gathered strip of cloth used as a trimming.

SEAM ALLOWANCE The narrow strip of raw-edged fabric that is left on each side of a stitched seam.

SEAM LINE The line formed when two pieces of material are stitched together.

SILK A luxurious and soft yet strong fabric produced from a fiber spun by silkworms.

STRUT A bar in a lampshade frame designed to brace and strengthen it against pressure.

TEMPLATE A shape cut from cardboard or paper and used to mark specific outlines on fabric.

TICKING A striped, closely woven heavy cotton twill fabric, usually with a thin stripe.

TOILE DE JOUY Cotton cloth printed with pastoral scenes in a single color on a neutral background.

TOPSTITCHING A straight seam seen on the right side of the fabric.

VALANCE A strip of fabric or a fabric-covered board that runs across the top of a window.

VELCRO A double tape used for closing fabrics. One piece of tape is covered with a synthetic fuzz while the other is covered with tiny nylon fiber hooks. When pressed together, the two fabrics cling together until they are torn apart.

VELVET A plush, luxurious warp-pile fabric with a short, closely woven pile. Can be made from cotton or synthetic fibers.

VOILE A light, plain-weave cotton or man-made fabric. Suitable for sheer curtains and bed drapes.

WAIST The narrow, middle part of a lampshade, often used to accentuate a flaring or pleated skirt.

WEAVE An interlacing action used to form something, such as a fabric.

WIDTH The distance from selvage to selvage on any fabric.

directory of suppliers

PILLOWS

Calico Corners
800 213 6366
www.calicocorners.com

Chelsea Textiles
979 Third Avenue
NY NY 10022
212 319 5804
Trade only
www.chelseatextiles.com

Pierre Deux
Stores nationwide
888 743 7732
www.pierredeux.com

Pottery Barn
Stores nationwide
800 838 0944
www.potterybarn.com

Silk Trading
888-SILK-302
www.silktrading.com

HOME FURNISHINGS

ABC Carpet & Home
888 Broadway
New York
NY 10003

212 473 3000
www.abchome.com

Ad Hoc Softwares
136 Wooster Street
New York, NY 10012
212 982 7703

Bed, Bath, and Beyond
Stores nationwide.
800-GO-BEYOND or visit
www.bedbathandbeyond.com

Calico Corners
800 213 6366
www.calicocorners.com

Donghia Furniture/Textiles Ltd
485 Broadway
New York
NY 10013
212 925 2777
To the trade only
www.donghia.com

Gracious Home
800 338 7809
www.gracioushome.com

Pottery Barn
888 779 5176
www.potterybarn.com

Ralph Lauren Home
800-379-POLO
www.rlhome.polo.com

Restoration Hardware
800 910 9836
www.restorationhardware.com

John Rosselli
979 Third Avenue
New York
NY 10022
212 772 2137
To the trade only
www.johnrosselli.com

LAMPSHADES

Just Shades
21 Spring Street
New York
NY 10012
212 966 2757
www.justshadesny.com

Mainely Shades
100 Gray Road
Falmouth
Maine 04105
207 797 7568
www.mainelyshades.com

Oriental Lampshade Company
816 Lexington Avenue
New York
NY 10021
212 832 8190

Vaughan
979 Third Avenue
New York
NY 10022
212 319 7070
To the trade only.
www.vaughandesigns.com

FABRICS & TRIMMINGS

B & J Fabrics
525 7th Avenue (2nd Floor)
New York
NY 10018
212 354 8150
www.bandjfabrics.com

Brunschwig & Fils
979 Third Avenue
New York
NY 10022
212 838 7878
To the trade only
www.brunschwig.com

Lee Jofa Fabrics
800 453 3563
www.leejofa.com

M & J Trimming
1010 Sixth Avenue
New York
NY 10018
212 204 9595
www.mjtrim.com

Osborne & Little
979 Third Avenue
New York
NY 10022
(Also includes Designers Guild)
To the trade only
www.osborneandlittle.com

Silk Trading
800 854 0396
www.silktrading.com

Tinsel Trading Co.
47 West 38th Street
New York
NY 10018
212 730 1030
www.tinseltrading.com

Waverly Fabrics
www.waverly.com

VV Rouleaux
www.vvrouleaux.com

CURTAINS & POLES

Calico Corners
800 213 6366
www.calicocorners.com

Country Curtains
800 937 1237
www.countrycurtains.com

Ikea
www.ikea.com

Kirsch
P.O. Box 0370

Sturgis
MI 49091
800 528 1407
www.kirsch.com

Pottery Barn
888 779 5176
www.potterybarn.com

Restoration Hardware
800 910 9836
www.restorationhardware.com

Silk Trading
888-SILK-302
www.silktrading.com

BED LINENS

Bed, Bath, & Beyond
800-GO-Beyond
www.bedbathandbeyond.com

Bella Linea Nashville
6031 Highway 100
Nashville
Tennessee 37205
615 352 4041

The Company Store
800 285 3696
www.thecompanystore.com

Fortunoff
800-FORTUNOFF
www.fortunoff.com

Lassiter's Bed N' Boudoir
3500 Peachtree Road
Atlanta, GA 30326
404 261 0765

Pottery Barn
888 779 5176
www.potterybarn.com

800 876 3226
www.shabbychic.com

credits

Page 2 Pillows from The Blue Door

Page 4 (above) Lampshade made by Bella Figura, fabric from Baer &
Ingram, trimming from Jane Churchill; centre quilt made by Tobias and
the Angel; below voile from Cath Kidston
Page 5 Velvet piping from VV Rouleaux
Page 7 Fabric and fringe from John Lewis

BED LINEN
Page 8 Antique eiderdown from Tobias & the Angel
Pages 12–15 Piqué and gingham from McCulloch & Wallis
Pages 16–19 Linen fabric from Designers Guild, trimming from VV
Rouleaux
Pages 26–29 Quilt made by Tobias and the Angel
Pages 32–35 Fabric from Christopher Moore Textiles
Pages 42–45 Checked fabric from Ian Mankin, valance fabric from
Osborne & Little, corona from The Blue Door

PILLOWS
Page 50 Pillow from Harrods
Pages 54–57 Fabric from Chelsea Textiles
Pages 58–61 Bobble fringe from Jane Churchill
Pages 64–67 Fabric by Schumacher from Turnell & Gigon, tassel from
Wendy Cushing
Pages 68–71 Made by Hikaru Noguchi
Pages 78–81 Outer fabric from John Lewis, tassels from Wendy Cushing
Pages 82–85 Fabrics from Sanderson, ties from John Lewis
Pages 88–91 Fabrics from John Lewis

LAMPSHADES
Page 92 Shade by Sally Harclerode, fabric from Designers Guild, piping
from VV Rouleaux
Pages 96–99 Shade by Sally Harclerode, silk from Pongees
Pages 102–105 Shade by Bella Figura, fabric from Baer & Ingram,
trimming from Jane Churchill
Pages 106–109 Shade by Robert Wyatt, ribbon from VV Rouleaux
Pages 112–115 Fabric from Manuel Canovas, base and shade by
Vaughan
Pages 116–119 Shade from The Dining Room Shop
Pages 126–129 Shade by Vaughan, fabric from Ian Mankin, trimming
from VV Rouleaux, sconce from Vaughan
Pages 130–133 Shade by Sally Harclerode

CURTAINS
Page 134 Fabric from Designers Guild, rope trim from VV Rouleaux
Pages 138–141 Fabrics from Ian Mankin, trimmings from VV Rouleaux
Pages 142–145 Antique linen from Nicole Fabre, curtains by Reed
Creative Services
Pages 148–151 Fabric from Pierre Frey
Pages 152–155 Fabric and trim from John Lewis
Pages 162–165 Fabric from Designers Guild, rope trim from
VVRouleaux

index

acknowledgments

Producing a soft furnishing book of this magnitude requires not only a huge amount of fabrics, trimmings and other sewing paraphernalia, but also very special skills that produce the best finishes. I have had invaluable help from many fabric companies, all of which are listed in the directory of suppliers, who very generously donated many metres of fabric for the projects in this book. I have also benefited from the generosity of suppliers of lamps and shades, curtains poles and fixtures, beds and bedding, and cushion pads and covers. Thank you, one and all.

James Merrell's beautiful photographs are the making of a book like this, and I owe him a big thank you for his ever-professional input and unflagging energy. To make the pictures as inspiring and accessible as possible, we photographed the soft furnishings in real homes, and I am very grateful to the people who so kindly allowed us to disrupt their lives and hang curtains, throw cushions and scatter lamps and bedspreads around their houses. These include Isobel Bird, Liz Shirley, Anna Thomas, Susie Tinsley, Cath Kidston, Annie Stevens, Tim Leese, Bobby Chance and Fiona Wheeler – many thanks to you all.

Hänsi Schneider, Helena Lynch, Celia Dewes and Robert Wyatt have all been instrumental in the hand-crafting of many of the objects in this book—their work is exquisite and greatly appreciated.

Thank you to all at Ryland Peters & Small for another professionally produced book. The beautifully drawn illustrations that accompany the instructions are the work of Lizzie Sanders, Michael Hill and Jaqueline Pestell, each of whom has produced work of the highest standard— many thanks.

Janey Joicey-Cecil and Catherine Coombes have both enabled me to work freely due to their continued support, help, and friendship. You are both truly appreciated.

Dedication
For my goddaughter, Kate Joicey-Cecil, in celebration of your 21st year and wishing you a happy and fulfilled adulthood.